René Lauret, an eminent French journalist, is the author of several books (*Raymond Poincaré*; *Les Conditions de la vie en Allemagne*; *Le Théatre allemand d'aujourd'hui*; *Le Trois Grands et la bombe atomique*; *Faites travailler l'Allemagne*; and *Causes de guerre, chances de paix*). This is his first volume to appear in English. He studied at the Universities of Montpellier, Nancy, Paris, Leipzig and Munich, and was a professor in Le Havre and Paris. An interpreter in the British Army during the First World War, he returned to journalism and was President of the Foreign Press Association. During the Second World War, he was the Press Attaché in the French Embassy in Bern. An editor for the *Bulletin de l'Étranger* and on the editorial staff of *Le Monde* from 1944 to 1953, M. Lauret is now retired and lives in Paris. Among his many honorary awards are Officer of the Legion of Honor (France) and Knight of the Order of Merit, First Class (Germany).

FRANCE AND GERMANY
The Legacy of Charlemagne

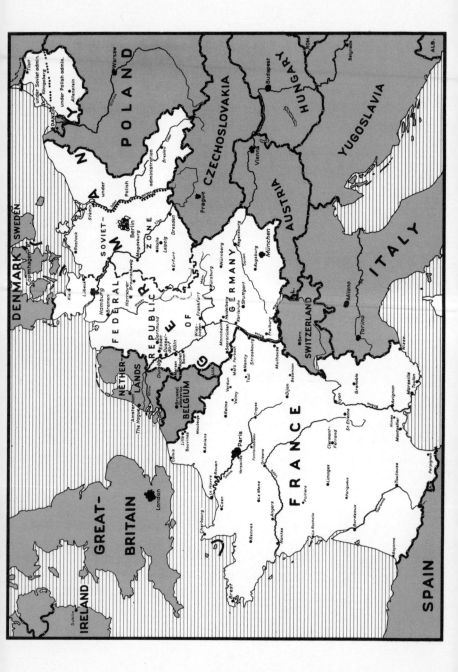

France
and Germany
The Legacy of Charlemagne

BY RENÉ LAURET

Translated by Wells Chamberlin

 HENRY REGNERY COMPANY
CHICAGO 1964

This translation from the original French,
Notre Voisin L'Allemand,
published by Nouvelles Editions Latines, 1960.

Le rapprochement amical de nos deux pays est sans conteste l'un des événements les plus importants et éclatants de tous ceux que l'Europe et le monde ont vécu au long des siècles.

—General de Gaulle
April 1962

Contents

Celts, Germans, and Romans

MANY centuries ago, two peoples, the Celts and the Germans, lived side by side in Germany—the former in the west and south, occupying the lands as far as the Weser and the Danube, the latter toward the lower Elbe and Jutland and probably extending eastward as far as the Vistula. These were the first Franco–German contacts.

According to Greek and Latin writers, whose statements go back to 500 B.C., these two peoples were unusually alike. "They can pass for brothers," wrote the geographer Strabo. For many years, Mediterranean peoples had difficulty in telling them apart.[1] The Teutons, whose name has become one of our synonyms for "German", were perhaps a Celtic tribe which the Cimbrians drove along with them when they invaded to the south. Marius crushed them at Aix-en-Provence.

1

The Celts, whom the Romans would call the "Gauls" *(Galli)*, after pushing into northern France, spread out, five centuries before our era, into most of the country.[2] Had they been driven from Germany by the Germans, or were they simply following that wanderlust which was to take them on to Great Britain, to Rome, to Greece, and to Asia Minor? The causes of the migrations of peoples are not completely clear.

The Gauls, conquered by Caesar, had ruled only a short time over Gaul before it became a Roman province. The Celtic tongue was replaced by Latin, and the land was Christianized. It is difficult to determine to what extent the French of today are descended from the Gallic invaders, to what extent they are descended from the older populations which the Gauls conquered but did not eliminate—Ligurians, Iberians, and others—and to what extent they come from the Romans, or from the Germans, who would be the last to arrive.[3]

At the time of the Roman conquest, the main body of the Celtic tribes appears to have settled in what is modern France, while most of the Germans had settled in central Europe. We use the term "tribe" because there was never, then nor later, any Celtic or Germanic state or nation, but rather scattered tribes, fighting among themselves, moving about independently, German against Celt or each against others of his own group.

It was a fortunate thing for its inhabitants that Gaul was conquered by Rome. "Gaul was about to become Germania," said Michelet. The Germans were threatening it as early as

Caesar's time. Indeed they threatened not only Gaul, but the Roman Empire itself, and the emperors were forced to send powerful expeditionary forces beyond the Rhine, which were not always victorious. Had the Germans then conquered Gaul, it would not have known Roman civilization and would have been Germanized.

In the fourth and fifth centuries A.D. when the Germans, the Burgundians, the Visigoths, or the Franks invaded Gaul, they found, as they had throughout the empire, peoples who were less warlike than they and who apparently offered them little resistance. Perhaps the Gallo–Romans had been lulled to sleep by the *pax romana*, which might be considered one of the great causes of the fall of the empire.[4]

Although the German invaders were able to establish ephemeral kingdoms everywhere, only the Franks were capable of holding them, and it was not long before the conquered populations absorbed the conquerors. This may be an indication that the invaders were relatively few in number and could have been resisted. The main body of the German people must have remained east of the Rhine, since after the dividing of Charlemagne's empire a powerful German kingdom arose there, later to become the rival of France.

[1]This opinion may have been based on insufficient knowledge of the two peoples. It may be observed, however, that according to the descriptions of both, the Celts were probably tall like the Germans, although perhaps a little less so, with blond hair like theirs, shading sometimes to red, and with blue eyes. The Germans, at least the Franks and the Gauls, wore mustaches, while the ancient Greeks and Romans were either smooth-shaven or wore beards.

3

[2]The Celts probably occupied the lands between the Rhine and the Seine in the ninth century. They drove the Ligurians to the Pyrenees about the year 500 B.C., penetrated the Po Valley about 400 B.C., and reached the Mediterranean coast early in the third century B.C.

[3]Cf. Seignobos, *Histoire sincère de la nation française:* "French schoolbooks are wrong in teaching pupils that our ancestors, the Gauls, were tall and blond. These children are not descended from Nordic warriors, but from peasants who had settled earlier. All that we have the right to tell them is that their ancestors spoke the Celtic tongue introduced by those warriors."

[4]Of course many other causes have been discovered or imagined by the historians.

CHAPTER 2

The Franco–German Empire

IT is a rather commonly accepted idea that Clovis, a Merovingian Frank, founded the kingdom of France, and that another dynasty, or more exactly, its most famous representative, extended France's sway to Germany and to Italy. In other words, France is said to have annexed the two countries. In fact, however, Clovis was never king of France, but king of the Franks, a Germanic tribe which had come from the mouth of the Rhine, and this is something quite different. If these Franks, pushed by other Germans, had moved on towards Spain, Clovis would still have been their king. As it happened, he settled in France, after destroying the Burgundian and Visigoth kingdoms. He also ruled over a part of Germany, and conquered the Germans living in southwestern Germany. The Franks themselves were overflowing along a wide front onto the right bank of the Rhine.

For three centuries before the time of Charlemagne, the successors of Clovis sought to increase their holdings to the east, so that the kingdom of the Franks was, during this whole period, a Franco–German kingdom. Charlemagne put the finishing touches on his conquests by annexing the Saxons and the Bavarians. He added the north of Spain, Italy all the way to Rome, and had himself crowned by the pope as emperor of the west.

The Franco–German Empire which he is given credit for creating was in reality the work of the two Frankish dynasties which had reigned in France for more than four centuries. Charlemagne merely concluded this work, rounding out and organizing the territory of an empire which his grandsons would destroy by the Verdun division.

It is a rather curious fact that both France and Germany claim Charlemagne as their emperor. He is introduced to French school children as a French emperor, to German school children as a German emperor. We are both right, since he ruled over both Germany and France. Although he was a Frank, therefore a German, and preferred to speak the German language, his native tongue, and Aix-la-Chapelle was his capital, the true focal point of his empire, which included France and Italy, was incontestably in the Latin countries, which were larger and more heavily populated than the Germany of the time. This double claim, German and French, can be considered as evidence of the harmony which reigned for a time between the Latin and Germanic peoples.

6

One German alone found this suspect. Hitler criticized Charlemagne for his good relations with the Church and for having mistreated the pagan Saxons, better Germans in his eyes than the Franks who had collaborated with Rome. He tried unsuccessfully to impose this view of things, but even before his demise, official history in Germany was returning to the thesis of the great German, "Karl der Grosse," as the heir of Rome and the forerunner of the Holy Roman Empire.

Asking about what "might have happened if" is generally rather futile, but hindsight can sometimes help us understand history. One sometimes wonders if the western empire could have endured, supposing the descendants of Charlemagne had handed it down intact from father to son. Must the fall of the Franco–German state, which, we repeat, did not exist solely under Charlemagne and his first successor, but which had existed since the time of Clovis, be attributed to the incompatibility of the Germans and the Franks, as some historians would have it, or rather to the impossibility of governing a territory which was too big, with the Roman administration gone? These explanations do not appear to be sufficient. Charlemagne had established a rather strong administrative system. Diversity of peoples and languages did not play a large part at the time; when territories were divided, these factors were not taken into account.

The much larger Roman Empire included populations and languages which were much more varied than those of the empire of Charles. With the exception of soldiers, a few traders, and a few monks, people traveled very little in the new empire. What did it matter to the inhabitants of a Romance country that the Germanic tongue was being spoken a few leagues away? Moreover, it was still not a question of a French language and a German language, but of innumerable French and German dialects. A Frenchman from Champagne understood a Breton or a Gascon no better than he did a German. No one was able to read and write, unless it was the churchmen, and their universal tongue was Latin.

People sometimes think that France and Germany, after forming separate states, found themselves embarrassed at being united into a single one. But there had never been a France or a Germany. The inhabitants of what is France today had belonged to the Roman Empire before belonging to the Frankish Empire, and the latter could be considered as the natural successor of the former. The Germans had had many relations with Rome before its fall, and some of their tribes had been associated with the Empire. Germans served in the legions, and Ataulf, king of the Visigoths, was known to have married the sister of Emperor Honorius.

The national entities which were to emerge several centuries later did not then exist, and the Church, whose power had grown since the fall of Rome, was a far stronger bond among western peoples than any community of race or of language. Combined with the military power of the dominant people of the times, the Franks, it could hold together Germans, French, and others as well.

Modern states were created by political power, not by what later would be called nationality, community of race and particularly, community of language. Originally, almost all these states included men of different tongues. Every where the language which finally prevailed was imposed through political considerations. Furthermore, this evolution has not always been accomplished along the lines of a national state. Switzerland, Belgium, the Turkish Empire, the Hapsburg Empire, which became the Austro–Hungarian Empire, the Russian Empire, which became the U.S.S.R., India, and Indonesia were or still are states including different peoples speaking several languages. Switzerland, where German, French, and Italian are spoken, might be thought of as a kind of small-scale model of the Carolingian Empire.

It seems that the political fact which determined the division of that empire was merely a Frankish custom, which, from the time of Clovis to that of Charlemagne, had already divided the kingdom of the Franks at each change in rule. Like modern personal property, it was divided among the sons of the dead king. Each time, after going through many vicissitudes, it would be reassembled as well as it could be. But this custom, so contrary to the consolidation of a state and to its political continuity, would eventually be fatal to the empire.

The people did not ask for the Verdun partition. They had no say in the matter. The Franks were the masters in France, in Germany, and in Italy, and their sovereigns acted according to their own good pleasure. Let us not overlook the fact that this division destroyed their position in the three countries. The Carolingians in the west and their cousins in the east soon gave way to other dynasties which were no longer Frankish. In the western kingdom, corresponding to modern France *(Francia occidentalis)*, the Franks, sepa-

9

rated from the other Germans, soon melted into the Latin population. In the eastern kingdom, corresponding to Germany *(Francia orientalis)*, others of these same Franks, no longer enjoying the prestige of a people in control of a great empire, were no more than a Germanic tribe, one among many. Other tribes surpassed them and gave Germany its rulers.

The Franks, in dividing their empire, eliminated themselves as a historic factor, but they had founded a kingdom to which they left their name—France was the first state created in the period of Gaul's existence as a geographic entity. (Before Caesar, Gaul had been occupied by a conglomeration of tribes, Celts and others, and after Caesar it became a Roman province.)

A new dynasty, no longer Frankish, the dynasty of the Capetians,[5] would build this France during the course of eight centuries. But it was the Franks, from the first two dynasties of Clovis down to the descendants of Charlemagne, who had created it, gathering its populations into a single state. All of the countries conquered by the Germans were not so fortunate. Spain, for example, emerged from German domination only to fall under that of the Arabs, and Italy remained divided until the nineteenth century.

It can be admitted that the birth of German royalty and of French royalty distinct from each other marked the end of the great Germanic invasions and records their failure. As long as the Franks were ruling a large part of western Europe, the invasions, as a whole, can be considered as generally successful. Once the Germans confined themselves to that Germany from which they had set out and where their greater masses had remained, and once France asserted herself as a Romance land which was assimilating its conquerors, the conquerors made no more conquests. Their incursions beyond the Rhine are reduced to abortive attempts, except in England, where the Saxons would impose themselves, their language, and their customs.

The cause of this fiasco is to be sought only in the disorder which characterized the great movement we call the "big invasions" and which the Germans call the "migrations of peoples" (*Völkerwanderung*). When the empire broke up, the Germans were strong enough to take its place. They were then the great warrior people, and they were more numerous than the Romans had ever been, than the little tribe from Latium which had gradually expanded, joining politics and the force of arms, and multiplying by absorbing other peoples. The Germans, however, remained divided in their tribes, each acting on its own and all fighting with each other. If they had been placed under a single chief, as they were for a time in the Frankish Empire, they could have reigned over all of western Europe.

For France, the Germanic invasions had not been without advantages. As everywhere else in the west, they first substituted disorder for Roman order. The Franks did eliminate other Germans, or barred their passage. They supported the Church, which was the only civilizing force of the time. They repulsed the Huns, the Arabs, and other invaders. Contact with them and intermarriage with them brought new strength to a blood which had cooled and slowed in the veins of the

11

descendants of the Gauls and the Romans. As a result, the French would be able to defend themselves against the Normans, take part in the Crusades, and fight with all their neighbors, as custom and necessity dictated in those troubled times.

[5]The origin of the Capetians is a moot question. According to legend, the first of them, Robert the Strong, was a butcher's son. Are we to accept the legend or the story of the two chroniclers of the time, Aimoin and Richer, who say that this Robert was the son of a Saxon immigrant, Witikind? Considering the customs of the time, can we admit that the counts, barons, and other nobles who were in power would choose a butcher's son as sovereign? Even those who support this thesis admit that Robert's mother was probably a Saxon, from which it follows that he was at least half Saxon, as was the last of the Capetians before the Revolution, Louis XVI, whose mother was the daughter of the Elector of Saxony. A strange coincidence!

CHAPTER 3

The French and the Germans: Back to Back—and Face to Face

IF a good boundary had separated France and Germany, they would undoubtedly have had fewer quarrels. But are there any good boundaries? The Rhine has been called a good boundary, yet, we read in Tacitus' *Germania* that "when a tribe had become powerful, a river like the Rhine was no more than a weak obstacle for it." Big and little peoples, once they are neighbors, quarrel over border territories. Only the union of France and Germany within the western empire was able to make friendly peoples of them. Separated, they were destined to become enemies.

The division of the Treaty of Verdun had been made in three shares, since Charlemagne had three grandsons. A long strip of territory was marked off between France and Germany, running from the North Sea to Rome. It was called

Lotharingia, from the name of Lothair, who at the same time fell heir to the title of emperor. This geographic monster, giving us as it does a sorry picture of the political acumen of its creators, soon disappeared, since at the death of Lothair, each of his two brothers took a piece of the median strip. Nor did this new partition endure. The French Carolingian and his German cousin both wanted all of Lotharingia, and after many vicissitudes, it remained in the hands of the Germans.[6]

This did not occur without a counterclaim from France, which would be maintained for centuries, and which is the source of the Franco–German territorial dispute. As a matter of fact, neither France nor Germany had any more rights than the other to a territory populated by Germans, French, and Dutch. According to our modern concepts of international law, France might have laid claim to the French territories, Germany to the German, etc., but such concepts did not prevail in the tenth century. Germany and France quarreled over Lotharingia[7] because it had been a part of Charlemagne's empire and their kings on both sides considered themselves his heirs.

It is, nevertheless, a fact—perhaps a miracle—that for centuries this territorial dispute played no significant role. More than six hundred years elapsed before the Franco–German boundary was modified. The kings of France may simply have made the best of a boundary running along the Escaut and the Meuse and which was unfavorable to them. The kings and later the emperors of Germany did not seek to push further.

Let us give no credit to their peaceful intentions. France and Germany had only mild conflicts during the Middle Ages because they were busy elsewhere. During that period they lived back to back rather than face to face—Germany turning toward the south and the east, to Italy and the Slavic lands, France toward the west and toward England, not toward Germany.

It was during this period that Otto the Great, a strong ruler and good soldier, drove back the Hungarians, had himself named king of Italy, and seized the imperial crown (962), almost at the very time that the Capetians were definitively establishing themselves on the throne of France (987). The new emperor would reign over the German Holy Roman Empire, from which France would be excluded. The attempt to incorporate Italy into it turned the German sovereigns aside, toward the south, and involved them in endless struggles with the pope and with the Italian city-states, preventing them from attending to their German affairs. In the meantime, feudalism was growing stronger in Germany and would strip the sovereigns of their power. In the northeast, the Slavs were to be driven back foot by foot from the Elbe to the Oder, but this widening of the German area was halted prematurely by the empire's weakness.

Although France's vicissitudes during this period were no less stirring, the outcome was more favorable. Its kings too had to fight the feudal lords, but instead of capitulating to them, they would reduce them to submission. The evolution of France and Germany would take place along parallel lines, but lines running in opposite directions. Despite the

Hundred Years' War, French royalty would have in its possession a kingdom united and powerful, while the German emperor would let his power slip from his hands.

History records encounters, such as the Battle of Bouvines, which is said to have halted the German "invasion." As a matter of fact, the invasions of those days were generally no more than raids or pillaging forays; a few thousand men would take up arms, then hastily return home, since they could not occupy large areas. This victory of Philip Augustus was not won over Germany, but over England and over an all but fallen emperor, in favor of his rival. The king of France successfully intervened in the quarrel between the Hohenstaufen Frederick and Otto of Brunswick, who was set aside. Frederick obtained the crown and continued his friendship with Philip Augustus. This was the first Franco–German rapprochement.

How could this Germany have been dangerous for France? The decay of the empire begins with Frederick II, an emperor who was born and died in Italy, and who was more Italian than German. Less than a century later, at the time of Philip the Fair, a veritable reversal of power positions occurred. The emperor, considered the foremost sovereign of Europe, had to give way before the king of France, who was not yet encroaching upon him in the northeastern region, but rather in the area of the Saone and the Rhone, an area more or less attached to the empire. Lyon, an imperial city, became French in 1310; the Dauphiné became French in 1349, and the March of Burgundy or Franche–Comté—temporarily, it is true—in 1315. Provence, as part of the kingdom of Arles, had belonged to the emperor, and had been French since the days of Saint Louis.[8]

We find no German attack on France during the Hundred Years' War; perhaps this was because Germany was not strong enough to mount one.

When rivalry developed between the houses of France and Austria, Franco–German relations entered a more difficult phase. Certain historians have tried to read a Franco–German conflict into the long Valois–Bourbon struggle against the Hapsburgs. This, however, could be true only to a very limited degree. The policy of the French kings was precisely to remove the German princes from the emperor's authority, and since they had long since escaped that authority, the policy consisted in maintaining the situation, and, if possible, in aggravating it. The purpose was not so much to divide Germany, as has been claimed, but rather to weaken the Hapsburgs, whose strength outside Germany had increased.

When this rivalry, essentially a dynastic conflict, began, the Hapsburgs, who were at first elective emperors, succeeded in having themselves attached to the empire.[9] Since the independence of the German princes was an established fact, the imperial power was weak and was not used over the armed forces of the princes. The house of Austria held its power much less from the title and functions of emperor than from vast holdings it had acquired outside of Germany: Bohemia, Hungary, Northern Italy, Franche–Comté, the Netherlands, etc. These domains, larger and more populous than Germany, had attained their apogee when Charles V inherited the kingdom of Spain from his mother.

17

Charles V was said to have the ambition to rule the world. Certainly modesty was not one of his vices, but isn't the accusation applicable to any head of a powerful state, whether his name be Louis XIV, Napoleon, William II, or Hitler? Although Charles V was able to encircle France, and his armies were able to invade it several times, his domination lasted only a few years. He was attacked in the east by the Turks, and at home he had to cope with Luther's Reformation, which was splitting Germany into two camps.

He did not even wait for death to force the division of his possessions, too vast and too poorly balanced, and he executed his bequests with a notorious lack of skill. Instead of giving the Netherlands to his brother, who became emperor, he ceded them to his son, along with Spain. The Dutch, a Germanic Protestant people who could not get along with the Catholic Spanish, revolted against them and soon won independence. If they had been attached to the empire, they might well have remained in it—their country was known at the time as "Low Germany."[10]

It was during the reign of Charles V that for the first time in six hundred years, the empire's northwest boundary with France was changed. Henry II took over the three bishoprics of Metz, Toul, and Verdun, apparent evidence that the empire, hugely swollen in all directions, was, in fact, an enormous, impotent mass.

[6]The Treaty of Verdun was drawn up in 843; that of Mersen, dividing Lotharingia, was made in 870, and the seizure by Germany of the whole of Lotharingia took place in 925.

[7]After Lothair's death, the name "Lotharingia" no longer applied to all of his former realm, but only to its northern part; the rest formed Burgundy and the kingdoms of Arles and Italy.

[8]More precisely, it had been ruled by the French dynasty of Anjou since the time of Saint Louis, and was annexed to France under Louis XI.

[9]After 1440. This elective nature was never abolished, but with each change of reign, a Hapsburg would henceforth be elected, with the result that the empire became hereditary *de facto* if not *de jure*.

[10]Cf. Salvador de Madariaga, *Portrait de l'Europe:* "This paradox can be proposed, that if Charles V had at that time left to the emperor what was known as 'Low Germany,' there is at least some doubt that Holland and Belgium would exist today."

CHAPTER 4

The Treaties of Westphalia and German Unity

THE Treaties of Westphalia and the Pyrenees recorded, as early as the middle of the seventeenth century, the victory of the Bourbons over the Hapsburgs of Austria and of Spain. The first treaty has been and still is a controversial matter in both France and Germany.

Contemporaries paid little heed to it. Although some excellent historians give it a very minor importance, others have made of it the masterpiece of great politicians, who are said to have tried to take against a so-called German peril precautions which would be valid for all time. This thesis, brilliantly expounded by such writers as Jacques Bainville, has adherents in both France and Germany. According to it, the Treaty of Westphalia and the policy resulting from it may have blocked German unity. Thus the French nationalists came to the conclusion that this treaty and this policy should be praised to the skies, and that they have been unfortunately neglected since the Revolution. German nationalists blamed France for the delayed formation of their national unity.

We may safely ignore the danger which a united Germany could have meant for France at that time. The Treaty of Westphalia terminated the Thirty Years' War, which was simultaneously a civil, religious, and foreign war, marking one of the lowest, if not the lowest, point in Germany's history. The devastated and bankrupt land had lost a large proportion of its inhabitants. Beside the France of 1648 this Germany could not be a great power; it was a conglomeration of 343 principalities which, even if they had been grouped into a single state, could have given France no cause for alarm.

The treaty extended the rights of these principalities in reference to the empire—these were the German "freedoms" as they were then termed (but it was a matter of the freedoms of the princes, not of the people). Each prince could impose on his subjects the religion of his own choice, negotiate with foreign powers, conclude alliances, and make war, but not against the emperor. France, as guarantor of these freedoms, had the right to have a permanent representative on the Diet of Regensburg.

However exorbitant this constitution of the empire may appear to modern Germans, we must admit that it scandalized none of their ancestors. The German princes found it generally excellent, for the Treaty of Westphalia merely reinforced their prerogatives which had been quite extensive since the Middle Ages. It did not destroy a non-existent German unity. It is apparent that such a unity could not exist in the middle of the seventeenth century, if one considers the force of habit and the weight of privilege. More than three centuries earlier, royal power had destroyed these factors in France. If the German emperors had fought against feudalism as effectively as had the kings of France, German unity would have been achieved long before the Treaty of Westphalia.

This means that Richelieu and Mazarin were not the authors of the division of Germany. Their game was played against a situation which had long existed, and was intended to weaken still further the position of an already weak emperor. The game, moreover, was played not among nations, but among sovereigns. It wasn't a struggle between Germany and France, but between the Bourbons and the Hapsburgs, and the latter were less feared as heads of the Holy Roman Empire, over which they held tenuous sway, than as the rulers of many countries from Bohemia to Hungary, and from Italy to the Netherlands and Spain. Charles V had left the latter country to his son, but the Hapsburgs of Madrid worked hand in glove with those of Vienna, and Richelieu's troops fought Spaniards more often than Germans.

It is well known that French policy was directed, not toward the division of Germany, but toward the humbling of the house of Austria. Random remarks of Mazarin on the necessity of dividing Germany are sometimes quoted, but in his mind as in that of his predecessor, this was not so much an objective in itself as it was a means of weakening the Hapsburgs, hitting them in their traditional domain, the empire.[11] Nothing indicated that this method would be always indispensable—Austria might become the ally of France, and a united Germany might one day be a factor in the European balance of power. Other states, England and Russia, were already powerful and would have to be reckoned with.[12]

Eleven years after the Treaty of Westphalia, the decadence of the Hapsburgs was to enter a new phase when their Spanish branch was forced to sign the Treaty of the Pyrenees. France acquired several provinces, and the Spanish infanta married the young French king, Louis XIV.

It is logical to believe that after this double victory of the Bourbons, the hour for reconciliation with the Hapsburgs had struck; it is always at such moments that a long-standing quarrel can be brought to an end in the best conditions.

However, Louis XIV, whose ambitions would later include obtaining the Spanish throne for his grandson, did not delay in making war again in Germany. He was at war there for the greater part of his reign, and one may wonder if this was consonant with the spirit of the Treaty of Westphalia which had presumably based peace in Germany on the opposition between the princes and the emperor. Under pressure from the overly powerful king of France, these princes returned to the orbit of their traditional leader. The Diet, over which the king thought to bring his influence, broke with him, and all the German princes except the Elector of Bavaria joined the emperor against him. Later, during the campaign of the Palatinate, almost all would again turn against France, and again in the wars which followed. We must conclude

23

perhaps that nothing had changed in Germany after the Treaty of Westphalia, unless it was that the partisans of France, dwindling in numbers, were tending to make common cause with the Hapsburgs, whom they feared less than the Great King.[13]

Fifteen years before Louis XIV's death, however, there occurred a major event which upset the situation in Germany —the margrave of Brandenburg was crowned king of Prussia. If the emperor had to grant this kind of promotion to a mediocre prince, it may have been to reward him for services rendered against the king of France. Was the emperor, in the position in which the Treaty of Westphalia had left him, still strong enough to prevent the rise of Prussia, soon to transform the newly made king into a rival? A half century later, Germany, where a scattering of little states would theoretically hold the emperor in check, included two important states— Austria, whose sovereign was still nominally the head of the empire, and Prussia, whose king was struggling now for first place. The king was already powerful enough to conquer Austria as well as France, and to be treated as an equal with Russia and England. Neither Richelieu, nor Mazarin, nor Louis XIV had foreseen this development, and it must be admitted that it was hardly foreseeable. A treaty which has been modified to that extent soon becomes outmoded.

We may wonder if Louis XIV, just before his death, had not come to understand this, when he ordered his envoy to Vienna to initiate better relations with the Hapsburgs.[14] Perhaps it was too late for the emperor to be able to take up the reins again in Germany. At this point the question arises:

Wouldn't a Germany unified by Austria have been preferable to a Prussian Germany? The Austrians were a more sociable, less warlike people than the Prussians. An ancient dynasty, rich with its holding of foreign lands, was less to be feared than a young, avid state, whose land was poor, and whose subjects were particularly distinguished for their military talents. Couldn't a basis for agreement be found between Paris and far-off Vienna, still facing, as the Holy Roman Empire had done in its early days, the Slavic east and the Italian south? Such a peace was all the more to be desirable because Louis XIV, after the fall of the Stuarts, would involve France in a long struggle with England, a struggle at sea which France could not face while still fighting on the continent, and during which she would eventually lose her vast empire— Canada and Louisiana—or to put it briefly, North America.

Since the German checkerboard was upset by the rapid rise of Prussia, it was no longer a question of setting a host of princelings against the emperor, but of choosing between the two largest of his adversaries, whether to play the Austrian or the Prussian card. Either could be played all the way, or they could be played alternately: One could side squarely with Austria or with Prussia, or one could establish a policy of hesitation, preventing either from creating German unity. French policy favored the latter decision, in reality because of circumstances rather than as the result of any well-considered planning. When Louis XV, after opting for Prussia, decided upon the famous "reversal of alliances" of 1756, he did not have French public opinion behind him, and this opinion was already beginning to sense its own strength.

Up to the Revolution it would remain violently anti-Austrian, a situation which forced the royal government to moderate its policy of rapprochement with Vienna. In reality this was a policy of hesitation, and Vergennes was to act as arbiter in the Austro–Prussian conflict. A relatively happy conclusion by French diplomacy before 1789, it left undecided, however, the question of German unity, together with all the explosive elements it contained.

The conditions which might have permitted this unity to be achieved existed no more in Germany than in France. Division continued inside the empire. Each one, the emperor, the king of Prussia, and all the princes, big and small, worked for himself, to maintain himself in power and to grow larger at the expense of his neighbor. To no one did it occur to renounce even a portion of his rights in favor of a great German state. The king of Prussia, whatever progress he may have made in less than a century, could stand against Austria but was not strong enough to eliminate her. Even after the Revolution and Napoleon, this Germany, shaken by great events and freed of most of its little sovereignties, was incapable of unifying itself.

[11]A traditional, not a hereditary domain, since the empire was still elective.

[12]A little later, in 1728, Montesquieu, traveling in Germany and observing the weakness of its constitution, expressed the wish that she might gather all her forces into a confederation. If such was the thinking of one of the best minds of his time, then all the French did not consider the division of Germany as dogma.

[13]Again, it is Montesquieu who tells us how Louis XIV's character hardly permitted him to win over the German princes: "Louis worked only toward arousing Europe's jeal-

ousy against himself; he seemed to have conceived the project of worrying Europe rather than conquering it. He seemed to have strength only for ostentation, and everything about him suggested the braggart, even his policy. Wars made often for no reason made people think that all those he waged later were equally unjustified. He learned neither how to start nor how to end his wars."

[14]His instructions were: "To form between the house of France and the house of Austria a union as advantageous to their interests as the maintenance of the general peace of Europe shall require."

CHAPTER 5

Frederick, "That Great Frenchman"

IF France was truly unable to choose between Austria and Prussia, this may have been because its government no longer had that unopposed authority which Louis XIV enjoyed. When it declared itself, and rather courageously too, in favor of the Austrian alliance, French opinion had become so infatuated with Prussia and with King Frederick that when he defeated the French army at Rossbach, the French general was lampooned in Paris. Twenty years later, French volunteers would be leaving for Berlin to enter the service of the Prussian king.[15]

Are we to believe that this public opinion, dominated all at once by habit, by passion, and by abstract ideas, gave evidence of a paucity of political sense? It accepted as a philosopher a king who perhaps was one, after his own fashion, but who made a complete mockery of philosophers—a king whose only law was to increase Prussian power at any price. It is true that he was host to Voltaire and that he rhymed in French, scorning the German language and literature. After his death, the thirty-one volumes of his works, written in French, had to be translated into German.

As the sovereign of a state which was still mediocre and poor, Frederick dominated his time; his mind and his culture, his devotion to the state he headed, his political and military genius, made of him a unique personality. Certain traits of his character, certain of his acts, were much discussed. He has been reproached for his offhand manner, his overfamiliarity, his cynicism, even for duplicity, which are not rarely found in statesmen and rulers.[16] Bismarck thought he detected a certain vanity in him, but men of all classes and all categories are not always free of it. He has been criticized for having taken Silesia from poor Maria Theresa, who did not hesitate to become accomplice in the division of Poland with Catherine of Russia, a much more serious affair. After all, Silesia had been a German province for several centuries, and Frederick and Maria Theresa were both Germans.[17] The division of Poland was a regrettable and indeed scandalous operation, consonant none the less with the practices of the time, and eventually it would prove fatal to Germany.

Later, after the awakening of German nationalism, the poet Arndt wrote: "We Germans, although we consider ourselves a people, must not take pride in this king. Not a one of us has done more evil."[18] But this king who never considered himself German—only a Prussian—had charmed both the Germans and the French. Goethe, brought up in the imperial city of Frankfort, notes in his *Memoirs* that the victorious Frederick had at least half the Germans for him.

This Prussia, whatever criticisms we may rightfully make of it, seems to appear in the perspective of German history as one of the rare successes. Charlemagne's empire, the Holy Roman Empire, the Austro–Hungarian Empire, and the empire of William I and of William II were brilliant failures; the Weimar Republic and Hitler's Third Reich were dull failures. One might say that the patient, economical principles of this kingdom, concerned with maintaining strict order in its states, were gradually extended through war and politics into an amorphous and changing Germany, and that the kingdom grew in the way Rome had grown. The Prussian methods were not so different from those of the Capetians, who had richer resources to work, a territory which was larger from the very beginning, and a larger population. Although the Prussian character is not that of the Parisians, the people of Marseille, the Bavarians, or the people of the Rhine valley, it nevertheless has its merits. It is in a city like Berlin that it can best be judged, the city which was transformed with astonishing ease from the capital of Prussia into the capital of a great Germany. The open, critical mind, the firmness, the courage, and the independence of Berliners have always impressed foreigners.

About 1830, the English writer Bulwer–Lytton would say, after visiting Prussia, that it was the best governed state in Europe, and, a little later, Edgar Quinet, a highly critical observer of Germany and the Germans, wrote: "Prussia has shown herself to be the truly innovating state of modern

times . . . We are being converted to its military institutions
. . . The Prussian system presupposes a very vital public spirit,
a patriotism which is moving toward a great goal . . . Between
it and the people there is a secret understanding for putting
off their liberty and for working together to increase the fortunes of Frederick."

Was Frederick, whom Michelet calls "that great Frenchman," a Prussian? He was by his education, by a tradition
which he inherited as the king of Prussia, and by the responsibility he assumed as sovereign, managing exclusively the affairs of Prussia, and against France, if need be. But the French
historian, in favoring him with that adjective, was thinking
no doubt of his taste for the French language and literature
and of his relations with famous Frenchmen. Did he know
that Frederick's very origins make him a Frenchman in the
proper sense of the term, a man of French blood through the
majority of his ancestors? It is a little-known fact, both in
France and in Germany. The genealogy of kings is certainly
no secret, but can the Germans be happy over the fact that
the greatest of their kings was a Frenchman? Can the French,
who were to make of Frederick the typical cynical, brutal
Prussian, admit that this particular Prussian was one of their
people?

For greater detail, we refer to the genealogy of the
Hohenzollerns which is readily available in a number of
sources. Let us simply recall here that the ascendants
of Frederick II are known without any lacunae at least to the
eighth generation. At that level the number of ancestors normally reaches 256, if there have been no intermarriages.[19]

France and Germany

Since such marriages are generally numerous in royal families, the figure is reduced in the present case to 117, and to 198 instead of 512 in the ninth generation. Among Frederick's ascendants, we find: 79 Germans (less than half the total), 4 Dutchmen, 1 Dane, 2 Englishmen, 2 Czechs, 4 Poles, 7 Scotchmen, 1 Spaniard, 1 Italian, and 97 *Frenchmen* (or about half of Frederick's ancestors). If we go back two more generations, we see that at the eleventh, he has three times more French ancestors than German, among them Admiral Coligny, the mother of Princess Louise of Orange, Eléonore Desmiers d'Olbreuse (daughter of a gentlemen of Poitou, who married the duke of Brunswick), and a large number of French generals, statesmen, and writers. Through James I, the son of Mary Stuart, Frederick descended from the famous queen of France and of Scotland.

It is hardly surprising that with such a family heredity, Frederick had French inclinations and affinities; yet they never influenced his policies. Contrary to modern men, he was always able to distinguish carefully between cultural and political nationalism. That there might be connections between the two never occurred to him, perhaps because Prussia was not a nation, but merely a state. This way of looking at things has been maintained at times in an aristocracy in which the taste for French language, literature, and art is found side by side with pronounced Prussian feelings.

The era of Frederick and of Maria Theresa is no doubt the last when French policy still had the choice of staking all on Berlin or on Vienna. Perhaps it was even then too late for such a choice. We have referred to the hypothesis according to which an old monarchy like that of the Hapsburgs might have offered fewer dangers as an ally of France. Nothing prevents one from supposing that the Prussian card might have been played. Although Frederick was more cunning, audacious, and unpredictable than Maria Theresa and her son, Joseph II, he was not eternal and his successors were rather mediocre.

In the complex policy of the king of Prussia there was more than one point of contact with French policy. These points of contact might have been exploited, provided he found what he wanted in them. That was no obstacle. The kings of France are not generally known to have been in the habit of working for others, or, as the popular saying goes, for the king of Prussia.

The fact that Prussia was not a secure power like Austria, and Germany was still a shapeless, fluctuating mass, offered even an exacting sovereign means of compensation. There were pro-French feelings in Prussia, as there were pro-Prussian feelings in France. What Prince Henry of Prussia, Frederick's brother, said after a trip to Paris may have been an invitation to France: "When this country wishes, it will always be capable of undertaking great things. But it is overly concerned with the love of peace."

Some years later the Revolution would remove this love of peace. France, as well as Prussia, Austria, and all of Germany would be in the throes of war for a quarter of a century.

[15]The absence of nationalism, in the modern sense of the word, in the sovereigns of the eighteenth century and in their subjects, cannot be overemphasized. Germans and Swiss were still fighting in all the armies of Europe. Condé, a prince of the blood, had fought on the side of the Spanish against his king. The best general of the imperial armies opposing

Louis XIV was Prince Eugene of Savoy, the son of a niece of Mazarin, born in Paris and raised at the Court of Versailles. And in the eighteenth century, Louis XV would make Maurice of Saxony, son of the elector, a marshal of France.

In 1791, the count of Narbonne, minister of war, offered the command of the Revolutionary armies to the Duke of Brunswick, a Prussian general, who three months later would lead the Prussian army against France.

[16]Frederick to Emperor Joseph II (1769): "You believe me full of bad faith, I know, I have deserved this accusation a little; circumstances required it, but that has changed."

[17]"Maria Theresa had not given in without many protests and lamentations. She consoled herself by taking the fattest prize, Lemberg and Galicia, with two and a half million inhabitants." (Pierre Gaxotte, *Fréderic II*)

The fact must be recognized, however, that the Austrian queen resisted the overtures of Frederick and the czarina for more than six months. After the first division of Poland (1772), she wrote to her son Ferdinand: "The danger of being along in a war against Russia and Prussia, the poverty, hunger, and sickness in my states have decided my involvement in this fatal negotiation, which is the shame of my reign."

Frederick had no such scruples.

[18]Arndt would write in 1806: "This (Prussian) monarchy was foreign to all that is German. It still is . . . Frederick reached his goal, which was to cast suspicion upon Austria and to weaken her, but he also suceeded in paralyzing Germany forever."

Others have reproached Frederick for having prevented Austria from taking back Alsace and for having set the German boundary on the Rhine. In his *Histoire de mon temps* (1746) we read: "All you have to do is pick up a map to be convinced that the natural limits of this monarchy seem to extend to the Rhine, the course of which seems purposely formed to separate France and Germany, to mark their limits and to serve as a terminal point for their domination."

[19]Perhaps we should remind those who might have forgotten or who have not thought about it, that the number of one's ancestors doubles with each generation that you go back—two parents, four grandparents, eight great grandparents, etc.

CHAPTER 6

Revolution and National Awakening

THE French Revolution marks the end of a long chapter in the history of Franco–German relations. And a complicated history it is, if it is true that a France which identified itself with French royalty faced a Germany which did not identify itself with the empire. For centuries the emperor had reigned but had not governed. Although his power extended to countries outside Germany, Germany itself, divided among countless sovereignties, from the nation of Prussia to the free cities and the canton-size principalities, escaped, for all practical purposes, from his control. Prussia was already denying him primacy inside Germany.

One cannot claim that during the period of almost a thousand years from the Treaty of Verdun to 1789 there was, properly speaking, any Franco–German quarrel. It was rather a case of rivalry between the French royal house and the empire, a rivalry which remained barely evident for centuries. The prestige of the sovereigns has a large place in it. This rivalry was aggravated when the Hapsburgs, having established the empire in their family, added vast personal domains to it through marriages.

The observation of Louis XV, stopping in front of the tomb of Marie of Burgundy in the Cathedral of Notre Dame of Bruges has often been quoted: "There is the cradle of all our wars." If the marriage of the heiress of Burgundy to the heir of the Hapsburgs was the principal cause of the hostility between the houses of France and of Austria, probably it was not, as has been claimed, because of German unity or the left bank of the Rhine that these illustrious families fought so long with each other, but rather because of the Netherlands, which belonged to the Burgundian heritage, and on which the kings of France had long had designs.[20]

Through its struggles with the empire, France did not conquer the Netherlands, except for a small part of Flanders, but it did take over successively the three bishoprics, Alsace, Artois, Franche–Comté, and Lorraine. It does not seem to have been inevitable that these conquests of fragments of old Lotharingia would lead to serious territorial conflict, with national feeling producing claims by both peoples. The possibility existed of reaching agreement through compensation or exchange. Although France had taken German Alsace, the empire held Walloon Belgium, and these provinces could have been exchanged. If not, France would simply have retained a piece of German land, and the empire a French area. The two things came out even.

In 1789 France was on good terms with Austria and Prussia. French opinion inclined toward Prussia, but Louis XVI, grandson of a Saxon sovereign, was the emperor's brother-in-law. A policy of prudence, which would leave Germany to itself or intervene there only discreetly, could still let her work out her unity as she saw fit.

One wonders if the Revolution was capable of developing a German policy. On the one hand, by advocating the revolt of peoples against rulers, it destroyed the old rules which had governed international relations; on the other, it declared itself faithful to the anti-Austrian tradition, which the French monarchy had tried to overcome. A contradictory attitude, at the same time innovating, but more reactionary than that of the monarchy which was being eliminated.

"The alliance of 1756 with Austria," Brissot exclaimed, "is incompatible with the French Constitution." "Prussia is our natural ally," declared Danton. In fact, both Prussia and Austria looked upon the revolutionaries as annoying trouble makers, and although it was the Legislative Assembly which took the lead in declaring war on "Francis II, king of Bohemia and of Hungary,"[21] the new king of Prussia, Frederick William II, who held revolutionary France in horror, did not hesitate to march against her.

How could two opposing policies be carried out—war on kings in general, and peace with the king of Prussia in particular? Either of these policies would doubtless have been possible—alliance with Prussia, or with Austria, on condition that all propaganda would be given up, and that it would be proclaimed that the Revolution was a purely French matter,[22] or a policy of "liberation" of the German people, predicated upon France's being clever enough to win them over, and strong enough to eliminate the princes. Revolutionary France won great victories, but they were still not great enough to set aside all the German princes, and France was unable to win the German people's favor, or at least was unable to keep it.

There was in Germany a certain enthusiasm for the ideas of the Revolution. The first revolutionary events had been acclaimed, particularly by the opinion of the intellectuals. A large proportion of the bourgeoisie was liberal. However, the death sentence against Louis XVI, and the dictatorship of the Terror were to incite against revolutionary France even those Germans who were most favorable to her.

In the Rhenish area, occupied by France, the inhabitants at first liked the reforms which were granted them; they participated with French officials in the administration of their country, and fought in republican and imperial armies. This feeling did not last. It was worn away little by little, as the conquerors turned into masters.[23] The conquerors may have fallen victim to the ease with which they had conquered. The French armies, more inspired and better led than those of the adversary,[24] had met little resistance. Yet the temptation of victory is conquest, and conquest leads to domination. After taking the left bank of the Rhine easily, France annexed it, instead of granting it independence, a gesture which might have tempted other German provinces, making them favor France. French departments were created here, and Napoleon would extend them all the way to Hamburg and Lübeck. Thus important sources of good feeling were wasted, and perhaps great possibilities as well, for German countries could become liberal, republican, even revolutionary, but only by remaining German. They had no intention of becoming Gallicized.

Could Napoleon, at the height of his power, attempt the reorganization of Germany, which had been too great an undertaking for the revolutionaries? For several years, from Austerlitz to the Russian campaign, he was the uncontested master of Germany. He suppressed the Holy Roman Empire, and the Hapsburgs no longer had any rights other than to the title of emperor of Austria. He enlarged certain states, reduced others, eliminated 253, made three kings (in Saxony, Bavaria, and Würtemberg), carved out the kingdom of Westphalia for his brother Jerome, and created the Confederation of the Rhine and thereby surrounded himself with satellites. And yet this Napoleonic Germany, made up of bits and pieces, counterbalanced only temporarily the two big states of Prussia and Austria, both of which he had hit hard, after demonstrating, in deference to the revolutionary tradition, a certain weakness for Prussia. A few victories which could only serve to bring the two rivals together against him had not settled their fate. Despite appearances to the contrary, this was merely a temporary situation, and it is to be supposed that Napoleon knew it. Germany was not, however, one of his major concerns at that time. His thoughts were turned toward Spain and particularly toward Russia. To neutralize one part of Germany and to siphon off manpower from the other was all that he could do to implement his master plan. The German game, half won, could not be completely won until Russia was conquered.

39

In the *Mémorial de Sainte-Hélène,* Napoleon asserts that he wanted to create a great German state which was to have been above the empire, Austria, and Prussia, "One of my great thoughts had been the massing, the concentration, of the great geographic peoples which revolutions and politics had dissolved or divided. Although they are scattered, Europe contains all told, 30 million Frenchmen, 15 million Spaniards, 15 million Italians, and 30 million Germans. I should have liked to have made of each of these peoples a single national body."

"It isn't that the Germans," he says on the other hand, "were not ready for centralization; they were all too ready, on the contrary . . . How did it happen that no German prince had judged the dispositions of his nation or had known how to take advantages of them? Assuredly, if God had made me a German prince, I should have governed 30 million united Gemans infallibly through the many crises of our times. And in the light of what I think I know of the Germans, if they had once elected me and proclaimed me, they would never have abandoned me and I would not be here."[25]

In that last sentence, Napoleon seems to be judging rather well the disciplined character of the German people. But he did not have time to carry out the policy he boasts of here (after the fact, of course). "All I did," he says, "was to simplify the monstrous complication of the German states." After his failure in Russia they turned against him, and the change was fatal. Some have thought to deplore the "treason" at Tauroggen, and that of the Saxons at Leipzig, but it may be more accurate to talk of "defections"—a man betrays his country, and the Germans were not French. Many times conquered, burdened with heavy taxes, stripped of important territories to the advantage of France, why should the German states not have seized the opportunity to throw off a foreign domination which they had endured and not desired? The fact that some among them had allied themselves to Napoleon, had followed him out of self-interest or fear, was small reason for their putting France ahead of Germany.[26]

Prussia, cajoled by the French up to the very eve of Jena, was to play the major role in the war called the War of Liberation. Leipzig, the generals Scharnhorst, Gneisenau, and Blücher, Queen Louise, the ministers Stein and Hardenberg, the philosopher Fichte, the writers and poets such as Arndt, Körner, and Rückert, are all German names, most of them Prussian, which we associate with the wars of 1813–1815. These wars united the whole German people for the first time, and the union was made against France. They had unified the German people, not yet in a single state, but there was a common feeling and Germans bore arms together. This is an event of immense implication—German nationalism was born as a reaction against the French nationalism spawned by the Revolution.

Unlike Louis XIV, Napoleon did not leave only bad memories in Germany. He remained relatively popular there, perhaps because Germans have a weakness for strong personalities. It was not he who created the revolutionary movement; he was only its instrument, the executor, and the shock from which German nationalism would rise up was due less to the Napoleonic conquests than to the propaganda of ideas and feelings. By substituting the nation for royalty (we know that the word "nation" was widely used at the time), by calling the whole people to arms, the Revolution transformed war, which had been the concern of sovereigns, into a national concern. From that time forward, it would no longer be kings or emperors facing each other, but peoples. The road to Franco–German conflict now lay open.

[20]Originally the Netherlands included in addition to the present-day Netherlands, or Holland, the larger part of what has become Belgium.

[21]Notice this formula, which avoids mentioning the German people, the empire, and particularly, the title of emperor, held by Francis as well as the titles of king of Bohemia and Hungary.

[22]The revolutionaries of 1848 would do this. They began by reassuring the foreign powers, telling them that they would abstain from any outside intervention. Thus they avoided foreign complications. They had learned from experience. Perhaps this kind of attitude would have been more difficult in the explosion of 1789; yet the Republic of the United States had just been founded on the principle of liberty for it, not for all peoples.

[23]In his great study, *L'Europe et la Révolution française*, Albert Sorel shows authoritatively, down to the smallest details, this change in German feeling toward France which occurred during the Revolution.

[24]And also bigger, if we can believe Napoleon.

[25]*Mémorial de Sainte-Hélène* (Pléiade Edition) II, pp. 483, 487.

[26]It may be of interest to note Napoleon's own opinion on this point: "What is quite striking in this matter," he says, "is that infamous acts remain basically foreign to kings, soldiers, and peoples. They are solely the work of a few sword-toting schemers, of a few reckless politicians. Not for a moment did I have any cause to complain of the individual princes, and the good king of Saxony remained faithful to me to the end." (*ibid.*, II, 190)

CHAPTER 7

The Franco-German Conflict

FROM 1789 to 1815, Franco–German relations had noticeably deteriorated. Between a country like France, where the great upheaval began, and a people like the Germans, seeking its own political framework, agreement was possible only if change was contained within France, or if the Revolution was universally successful, creating on both sides similar and associated regimes. It was easier for France to restore its relations with England, a more bitter enemy than Germany, but which was stable and had not been invaded, than with an unstable Germany, overthrown by invasion.

The nationalism which had caused the French people to rise up in 1792 had been answered in 1813 by a German nationalism. It may be said that the first was not directed against the German people, but against its princes. However, when the momentum of the French armies had carried them into Germany, German nationalism turned perforce against the invader. The alarming aspect of this is that the clash of the two peoples had produced claims on both sides.

The Revolution had pushed the claim of "natural boundaries," which had never been the policy of the French monarchy. One wonders if Louis XIV, had he been able, would have carried his boundary to the Rhine from Basle to Rotterdam. Although it was possible, he did not make a system of it. He adapted his policy to events, and the kings of France were always more interested in Belgium than in the Rhine. However, after Valmy and Jemmapes, when the Rhine had been reached, more easily than had been hoped, Danton extolled before the Convention the "natural boundaries" theme, and the press took up the cry. After various vicissitudes, the left bank of the Rhine, including Belgium, was to remain in French hands, and France's possession of these areas was recognized by the treaties of Campo–Formio and Lunéville. The Rhineland was divided into four departments which would be returned to Germany under the Treaty of Vienna.

If France was able to retain this province, certain conditions had to be met, and they were far from being met. The first was that France should stop at the Rhine, instead of pushing on into all of Germany. In so pushing on, she linked the Rhine to Germany's fate. It became evident that when France evacuated Germany, she would also have to give up the Rhine. Another possibility would have been to have helped Prussia or Austria to take over the direction of Germany. The Rhine would then have been payment for German unity, as Nice and Savoy were later to pay for Italian unity. But the Savoyards were French, and the people of the Rhineland were German, which makes an important difference. With national feeling inflamed, it is unlikely that the Germans would have admitted the loss of the left bank of the Rhine, as they had accepted the loss of Franco–Flemish Belgium when it was separated from the empire.

Their claims were not satisfied when they recovered what they considered as their property. They began to claim Alsace, and even Lorraine. Before the Revolution, pieces of the old Lotharingia had been fought over, as wars went, each people taking what it could, abandoning what it could not hold. This was neither a system nor a premeditated plan, and it was conceivable that a status quo would finally be established, and that it would be tolerated by both parties. In opposition to this solution, which was tantamount to the division of Lotharingia, France would now offer the theory of natural boundaries, which Germany rejected, claiming for its part the former lands of the empire. Between the two countries there extended from that time on a zone of dispute, where the conflicts of the future would arise.

These conflicts were to be sustained by much larger armies than in the past. The nation born of the Revolution would be entirely on a war footing. It could no longer be a matter of professional soldiers and mercenaries; both the defense of the realm and the conquest of the territories of others was the concern of everyone. After the first armies of the Revolution had driven the enemy to the border, those of the directory, of the consulate, and of the empire would swarm over Europe for twenty years.

The mass levy of troops, to which the Convention had resorted, would be regularized in 1798 by the Jourdan Act, organizing conscription. When Prussia, in 1813, took the leadership of the "liberation" movement, it employed the same methods and when the war was over, it decreed obligatory peacetime service. What for France had been only a wartime necessity now became an eternal necessity, one of the great institutions of the modern nation. (Restoration France reverted to the army of the *Ancien Régime.*)

Thus on many different areas, on feelings, on territorial aspirations, on military institutions, the Revolution left its deep marks. It had forged new things, and they were not of a nature to foster peaceful encounters.

The importance of the psychological change was not always understood by its contemporaries, particularly in France. Historians are inclined to attenuate it. Relations between the French and German governments in this period were proper enough. In France it was the time when a portion of public opinion was the most Germanophile. Victor Hugo, for example, in *Le Rhin,* was pro-German in an almost provocative way: "The author of this book has an almost filial feeling for that noble and holy fatherland of all thinkers (Germany). If he were not French, he would want to be German." Lamartine answered the author of the *Rheinlied* with his *Marseillaise de la paix.*[27] Many Romantics, among them Gérard de Nerval, the translator of Goethe's *Faust,* were fervent admirers of Germany. Certainly Mme de Staël set the tone for a whole generation in her famous work, *On Germany*, in trying to reveal "a people she did not know well to the French who did not know them at all."[28]

It is difficult to believe that these sympathetic feelings in the literary world corresponded to the deep feeling of the country. Musset, with his *Rhin allemand*, probably explained the mass reaction better than Lamartine had done. A few years before, Stendhal had written: "Two hundred thousand young Frenchmen are impatiently awaiting the opportunity to take up arms again."[29] And the British minister, Lord Palmerston, on his way through Paris, asserted that "all the French are losing their heads, and all would give their two hands to get the Rhine back." Even if we grant that the Englishman was exaggerating, that his "all" should be reduced to "some," this is evidence that the "mystique" of the left bank of the Rhine, if we may call it that, was alive in certain milieux in France. Napoleon III would not forget it. He would certainly have reannexed the Rhine if the outcome of the Franco–Prussian War of 1870 had been different.

And so then, the French position in respect to Germany was full of nuances. It allowed for feelings which were quite different, even contrary, and which sometimes co-existed in the same individual. If one expressed a contestable claim, it was on a note of sympathy. People claimed what they thought was their right, but what nation doesn't think it is in its rights when it is making a claim? The French, moreover, did not feel humiliated by the defeat at Waterloo; they had lost the final battle, but they might just as well have won it—at least that's what they thought. Nothing could efface the epic of which

Napoleon was the hero, nothing could efface the punishment he had meted out to all of Europe, including Germany. Louis XIV may have been rotten with pride, but he was none the less the great king celebrated by Voltaire, and France was still the great nation. We cannot say that the French suffered at the time from any inferiority complex. Nor did the Germans, apparently; they were often betrayed by their arrogant, insistent tone. France, although conquered, was still united, and Germany was not yet united. The victory of 1815 was not enough for her. Aspiring to victory, the German people received a hybrid constitution, which allowed the former divisions to remain, and the Germanic Confederation, which replaced the Holy Empire, had no real authority. The struggle remained unresolved between Prussia and Austria for predominance in Germany. For those who could read the signs, however, Prussia already was winning, through the power of its institutions, and the momentum and the hardness of its national spirit.

It is difficult to believe that alone among the French, only the historian Edgar Quinet saw this. In any case, he saw it more clearly than anyone else and expressed it in prophetic terms as early as 1831, thirty-nine years before the Franco–German War:

> The memories of 1814, and the joy of having been caught up in the world's motion created a love and a taste for political action. Prussia, an irritable and angry nation, wants to take back Alsace and Lorraine. Unity is the thought, deep, continuous, necessary, irrevocable, which is at work in this country and is cutting through

it in all directions. Religion, law, trade, liberty, despotism, all that lives here, all that thinks, all that acts, is driving in its own way toward this outcome.[30]

Those few lines tell the whole story. Prussia was interpreting German ambitions, and Prussia was ready to act in order to obtain satisfaction for them. Those ambitions were on the one hand, the creation of a united Germany, of a great Germanic state, and on the other, the recovery of Alsace and Lorraine, the provinces which belonged to the Holy Empire.

Following the stages of the Zollverein (or customs union) of 1833, the Frankfort Assembly of 1848 (a failure, but important because of its aftereffects), the Prussian campaigns against Denmark in 1864 and against Austria in 1866, and the formation of the North German Confederation under the aegis of Prussia in 1867, *it was evident* that Germany was taking great strides toward unity. Only the southern states, comprising fifteen per cent of the German population, were not included, and they had promised their aid in case of war. With the addition of a title and a supplementary crown, the new empire would be born, and the European powers, with the exception of France, would accept it. France, thinking to block the inevitable event, sought alliance with Austria. But Austria, defeated at Sadowa and courted by Bismarck, who took no territory from her, would not dare risk another defeat, and would desert France at the last minute.

It was the question of unity, rather than the question of the left bank of the Rhine, which mobilized French opinion behind Napoleon III in the years preceding 1870, when he was preparing for war against Prussia. A half-century after

1815, it was not easy to stir up the people in favor of a conquest of German provinces. But the struggle against German unity was certainly a tradition of French policy. It was still alive, if not among the people, at least among the heads of government, and consequently in the influential part of public opinion, which persisted in seeing in particularism an irreducible aspect of the German character—as if the tribal stage had not existed in the evolution of every nation, among the Celts as well as the Germans. Germany had simply been delayed in that stage, and this delay was to prove disastrous for all Europe.

Nevertheless, Napoleon III was fundamentally proGerman. Educated in an Augsburg lyceum, having many German relatives, he was, like his uncle before him, the partisan of a united Germany. Imbued with the principle of nationalities, he had been the artisan of Italy's nationalization. It took a particular combination of circumstances, certain blunders by him, plus Bismarck's will, to precipitate the catastrophe.

At first the establishment of the second empire had created a rather confused situation. The countries of southern Germany, where Napoleon was known personally, welcomed him, but Prussia looked upon him with mistrust. She refused to participate, as did Austria, in the Crimean War against Russia. After Solferino, she mobilized six army groups on the Rhine, which put an end to the emperor's warlike undertakings. After the annexation of Nice and Savoy, his "desires on the Rhine" were feared in Germany.[31] This has been a much-discussed matter and many ponderous works have been devoted to it by German historians.[32] Despite the many documents which were produced, the impression remains that it was probably a matter of more or less vague opinions rather than one of deliberate intent. The weak spot in Napoleon III's policy, growing ever more evident with his age and illness, had always been uncertainty and variability. Bismarck, after several conversations with him, had called him a "great unknown incapacity."[33] Very quickly he had based his game on Napoleon's defects.

It is not certain that he always wanted to make war on him. He wrote in his *Pensées et Souvenirs*[34] that it was inevitable, but he did not say at what point it seemed so to him —was it before the campaigns against Denmark and Austria, or only afterwards, when tension had increased between Prussia and France? Bismarck knew that the people's feelings do not always determine war, that these feelings are partly artificial, and that France, despite its claims to the Rhine boundary, had not attacked Germany since 1815. However, in the years immediately prior to 1870, Bismarck, in agreement with Roon, minister of Prussia, and Moltke, chief of staff, left nothing undone to improve an already excellent army, whereas a French marshall, the minister of war, thought he could win the war with gaiter buttons.[35]

During this period, Napoleon had made one false move after another, letting himself be fooled by Bismarck. On two occasions, he had offered an alliance to him which had been rejected. At one moment he was talking of annexing Belgium, at another it was the Palatinate or Mayence, or later, Luxembourg. The idea occurred to Bismarck to offer them to him, a highly impertinent gesture, since none of these territories was Prussian. Finally he revealed Napoleon's projects to the southern German states, who became indignant over them and could no longer refuse to ally themselves with Prussia. It is possible that war finally appeared inevitable both to Napoleon and to Bismarck. Shortly before the declaration of war, the emperor asked his prefects to undertake a survey of the state of mind of the population, and seventy-four out of eighty-nine prefects had replied that the people wanted peace. But the pressure applied by the empress and her clique, and the difficulties of a home policy requiring prestige successes were enough to incite him to go ahead. The rebuffs of Bismarck irritated him, and the rapid rise of Prussia after Sadowa worried him. He counted heavily on the alliances he had been negotiating for some months with Austria and Italy; they had not yet been concluded, and never would be.

The Ems Telegram, which oversimplifying historians have proposed as the cause of the war, was only a minor incident, a pretext furnished by Bismarck and eagerly taken up by his opponent. Bismarck wanted war to be declared on him; he did not want to have it declared by the king of Prussia, and perhaps in that case he could not have obtained the declaration. William I, seventy-three years old, was not, or at least was no longer, particularly bellicose; the goal he pursued was almost won and could be won without war. His alliance with the South German States was a purely defensive one, and he probably could not have counted on their help if he had appeared to them in the aggressor's role.

That is why, at the moment he was putting the finishing touches on the famous telegram, Bismarck observed to one of his accolytes: "It is absolutely necessary that we be attacked." Later he would admit: "I wanted to wave the red flag in the face of the Gallic bull." His calculations were accurate. The Gallic bull would charge, although one wonders if he really had to. Reasonable men did not think that the Ems Telegram, finely ground as it was by Bismarck himself, was worth a war. Thiers exclaimed from the rostrum of the Chamber: "I decline the responsibility for a war for which there is so little justification."

Indeed, before the Ems Telegram, hasty preparations were already being pushed forward for a campaign for which the country was not ready, militarily or diplomatically. On July 6, the prime minister, Ollivier, said to Prince Metternich, the Austrian ambassador, after a Chamber meeting: "We have decided unanimously to go to war. We have carried the Chamber, and we will carry the nation. Within two weeks we will have four hundred thousand men on the Sarre and we will wage war as we did in 1793." The Ems Telegram was sent on July 13, and war was declared on the 19th.[36]

[27]Nations, pompous word used for barbarity,
  Does love stop where stay your feet?
  Tear asunder these flags; another voice cries to you:
  "Selfishness and hatred along have a fatherland;
  Brotherhood has none!"

[28]A German woman much in the public eye at the time, Rachel von Varnhagen, judged Mme de Staël's work in these terms: "She has seen nothing, heard nothing, understood nothing. Her book is driveling nonsense."

[29]*The Red and the Black.*

[30]Edgar Quinet, *De l'Allemagne et de la Révolution.*

[31]Cf. Ernest Denis, *La Fondation de l'Empire allemand:* "It is not too great an exaggeration to say that for ten years, the inhabitants of the Palatine and the Grand Duchy of Baden went to sleep every night with the fear that they would be awakened the next morning by Algerian riflemen."

[32]Cf. particularly H. Oncken, *Die Rheinpolitik des Kaisers Napoléon III.*

[33]Bismarck also said about Napoleon III: "His intelligence has been exaggerated at the expense of his warmth of feeling. He is fundamentally a good man. He shows an unusual degree of gratitude for all that is done for him." (*Pensées et Souvenirs,* VIII, I)

[34]That war with France would follow the war with Austria was part of the logic of history, even if we had given Emperor Napoleon the small gratuity he asked for remaining neutral (*ibid.,* XX, II).

[35]Marshal Leboeuf, the minister of war, owes his fame to his statement before the Legislative Body on the eve of the declaration of war: "Should the war last two years, our soldiers won't lack a single gaiter button." Unfortunately, they did lack a number of other things, such as cannon and ambulances . . . and leaders.

[36]Let us review briefly the circumstances which preceded the Ems Telegram. A Hohenzollern, a distant cousin of the king of Prussia, had been a candidate for the throne of Spain, probably at the instigation of Bismarck. The French government strongly opposed this candidacy, and obtained satisfaction. Prince Leopold withdrew; this, in the opinion of such statesmen as Guizot, was a diplomatic victory for France.

It was then that Napoleon III charged his ambassador, Benedetti, to ask King William, who was vacationing at Ems, to promise that a Hohenzollern candidacy would never be proposed again. The king considered this request unacceptable, asked Benedetti not to insist on it, and dictated to his secretary the famous telegram, in which he reported to his prime minister what had transpired. Before giving it to the press, Bismarck revised and shortened it, giving it a tone which was found offensive in Paris.

It should be added that when Ambassador Benedetti was in Paris two days later, no one was curious enough to ask him for a precise and detailed account of his interview with William I, who had behaved most correctly with him, and who had informed him through his aide-de-camp that he would be happy if he came to greet him at the station.

In his book, *Vie espagnole de l'Impératrice Eugénie,* André Nevil says that Jules Cambon, shortly before his death, confided this to him: "I took advantage of my stay in our embassy in Berlin by rereading the records on the preliminaries of the war of 1870. Well, you might as well know that we were wrong."

CHAPTER 8

Might is Right

THE Germans, whether rightists or leftists, republicans or socialists, monarchists or fascists, revere Bismarck as the unifier of their country. The French, on the other hand, have sworn him an eternal hatred, perhaps greater than their hatred of Hitler.[37] It is difficult to explain this feeling particularly since Napoleon, who had trampled Germany for twenty years, is still rather well liked there. Bismarck has been turned into an uprepentant warmonger. Before the war of 1870, he had waged two small wars, against Denmark and Austria; each had lasted but a few days, while the war of 1870 lasted several months. For his part, Napoleon III's record shows three campaigns, the Crimea, Italy, and Mexico. Bismarck, who remained in power for another twenty years, engaged in no more wars. He was neither a soldier nor a conqueror, but a statesman with precise goals which he never overshot. He wanted to create German unity through Prussia; once this result had been attained, he had only one aim, to protect it and to consolidate it through alliances.

It is debatable whether three wars were indispensable to unify Germany, and whether it was in the interest of peace, or even in Germany's interest, to conclude an alliance with Austria, then another with Italy. When we think that in 1849 the Frankfort Assembly, which brought together deputies from all Germany, including Austria, had offered the imperial crown to the king of Prussia, we might be tempted to suppose that the German Empire could have been created without war. The king of Prussia refused the crown; perhaps he thought he could obtain it by other, more preferable means. But Bismarck was not the king of Prussia, and it was another thirteen years before he became its minister. In 1849 he had signed with a delegation which, in its petition to the king, begged him to accept the imperial crown.[38]

When Bismarck did come to power, he may have thought that the problem of German unity would be better solved by war. As a Prussian country gentleman, Prussian by temperament and tradition, he was no man to recoil from this extreme. He could not have failed to know that most nations had been created through war. Certainly it was by war that Napoleon III had just supported Italian unity, and that he had completed French unity by annexing Nice and Savoy. "France was made by the sword," De Gaulle has said. Why not Germany?

Since the Revolution, in order to control international relations, we have invoked great principles which should be substituted for the law that might makes right. Are these principles generally applied? Unfortunately, history, even today's history, teaches us that they are rarely applied. We go on hoping that someday they will triumph in the world. But in Bismarck's day it was not in the name of great principles that French opinion could lay claim to the left bank of the Rhine, which was German, and could oppose German unity. These claims could have triumphed only if the law of might makes right had been resorted to, and unfortunately for France, she was not the stronger. Her policy was beyond her capabilities. Bismarck's policy was that of a close-playing calculator, whose plans were always scaled to his strength. He had the quality, which many others had not had (Louis XIV, Napoleon, for example), of knowing how to judge his limitations. That is why he was successful where his French opponent failed. He is said to have coined the phrase, although he always denied it, "Might has primacy over right."[39] Although he may not have expressed it in precisely those terms, this maxim is thought to have influenced all of his policy. Yet certainly it will be recalled that La Fontaine, using long before Bismarck an old adage of popular wisdom, had said: "The reason of the stronger party is always better." Bismarck's mistake was to say aloud what everyone was whispering or thinking without saying it. In politics as in social life, hypocrisy is in order, cynicism is reviled, and Bismarck was the great cynic who did not respect the old rules of diplomacy.

Neglecting European history after the French Revolution, he also forgot that the principles it had spread, although they were still far from ruling the world, were alive, that many people still believed in them and that therefore it was unwise to come into conflict with them. When we conflict with them today, we are at least clever enough to add, "we are placing might at the service of right," or, "the other fellow is the aggressor."

The French remember among Bismarck's acts those which harmed their country, a normal reaction. Certainly, however, others served France—for example, his alliance with Austria–Hungary in place of which he could have made an alliance with Russia.

If we admit that the Triple Alliance triggered the system of counter-alliances which was to lead to World War I, we may think that a Germany without alliances might have been preferable. But the fact must also be admitted that Bismarck did not believe he could do without them, and a Russo–German alliance would have been much more dangerous for France than the Austro–German alliance. According to Bismarck's own statements, the Russian alliance was proposed by Shuválov in 1876 and again later, this time urgently. He realized that the Russian alliance would be stronger than the Austrian alliance, and that in addition it would block the alliance of Russia and France which appeared otherwise inevitable. Nevertheless he refused. The reasons he gives for the refusal are not very convincing. The Russian alliance would have been based essentially on the czar himself, who was yielding more and more to the influences of Pan-Slavism

France and Germany

(Pan-Slavism was directed less against Germany than against Austria–Hungary). Russia, by virtue of its size and its geographic position, would have had a marked superiority over Germany; extending over vast territories all the way to the ends of Asia, Russia might involve Germany in conflicts which would not be to her interest.

Strange as it may appear, Bismarck's preference for Austria, whose weaknesses he certainly knew, seems attributable to sentimental reasons as much as to those just cited. In his eyes, the empires of Germany and Austria–Hungary were German states, heirs of the Holy Roman Empire, and thereby having a close bond between them, a *staatsrechtlich* bond (a bond based on public law).[40] Little inclined by temperament to rely on the people, Bismarck nevertheless insisted on the popularity of the alliance among both the Austrians and the Germans.

This attachment to Austria dominated his policy. It certainly explains why he refused, after Sadowa, against the desires of his king and the military leaders, to annex any territory at the expense of the Austro–Hungarian Empire. It might also explain why, realistic though he was, he never thought of settling relations of the three empires over the corpse of the weakest of them—in other words to achieve that division of Austria–Hungary which was to be carried out in 1918. European diplomacy already saw this as a possibility. A less conservative statesman than Bismarck would have taken advantage of this combination of circumstances to enlarge his country, which lacked two German territories— Austria, from Vienna to Lake Constance, and the Sudetenland along the border of Saxony. The operation could have been carried out in a variety of ways—through annexation of the German territories, making of the rest of Austria–Hungary an almost entirely Slavic state, perhaps not a very viable one; through the annexation of all of this empire to Germany, bringing in strong foreign minorities, but leaving predominance to the German elements; or through a division of Austria–Hungary between Germany and Russia, giving the German provinces to Germany and dividing the rest into spheres of influence, with Hungary and Czechoslovakia falling into the German sphere, the rest of the Danube basin and the Balkans into the Russian sphere. The last solution would have been preferable for Germany, since it placed on its side the principal great power which might have taken offense at its aggrandizement. The aspirations of the small nations would have been satisfied, since several new states would have been created, in reality, as Russian or German satellites. One wonders if such an agreement could have been concluded before the Berlin Congress of 1878, where Bismarck, having already made his decision, supported Austria–Hungary against Russia. If the Russo–German alliance had not resulted until later, the division could have taken place when the influence of the two great empires, reaching from the Rhine to the Pacific, would have made all opposition by other powers impossible.

Instead of this radical solution, Bismarck chose one which was more complicated, consisting in incorporating into the Austrian alliance by a measure of precaution in order not to alienate Russia. He concluded with her the treaty called the

Reinsurance Treaty, by which Germany and Russia guaranteed their neutrality to each other in the case of an offensive war by France against the former or by Austria–Hungary against the latter. He hoped in this way to maintain the territorial status quo by limiting the risks which an alliance always contains.

This conservative policy, which could not be continued after his time, would one day result in Germany's ruin and in the destruction of the Austro–Hungarian Empire which he was unwilling to imagine, which he would have rejected indignantly had it been proposed to him.

When we consider the opportunities which were offered him and which he did not exploit, we must agree that Bismarck, whom historians have sought to present as a great militarist, as a conqueror, even as a kind of bogey man, was in reality a timorous statesman. What would have happened to France if he had played all his trump cards, if he had not been restrained by the traditions and the habits of the Prussian country gentleman and of the Prussian state, which was ambitious and stubborn, but narrow, and which did not have the larger view of things but was satisfied with a small Germany, much smaller than the Holy Roman Empire? These were also the traditions and habits of the inveterate monarchist, to whom the idea would never have occurred of despoiling an old dynasty like that of the Hapsburgs; and consequently, he was diametrically opposed to the Pan-Germanists, since Pan-Germanism desired the union of all Germans, which implied the destruction of Austria–Hungary.

For the Germans, Bismarck will always be the hero who created their national unity and for whom they had waited so long. It was he who at long last corrected the errors and omissions of a long history, who placed a great people on the same footing as others. His compatriots do not dream of reproaching him for the catastrophes which have come after him, even if they may be the results of his actions. Statesmen are not prophets, and they are not always responsible for the long-term consequences of their policies. It is not Bismarck's fault that his successors were William II and Hitler.

From Luther to Hitler, the men who played great roles in German history often had something harsh and brutal about them which one does not find in Latins like Caesar or Napoleon, or even in Robespierre. Bismarck also had great subtlety, which was not immediately apparent. His manners were hardly pleasing to the Germans themselves; they long opposed his policy, and it was not until his retirement, when they compared him to his successors, that they established any particular cult in his honor. In France he was considered a soldier, because he liked to wear the uniform and the spiked helmet. In reality, he enjoyed creating this image of himself, for he was quite the opposite, never having found the military profession attractive, and even displaying a certain scorn for those who were engaged in it.[41] Although his demeanor and his whole personality shocked the French, there are other reasons for their antipathy. For them he was not only the victorious enemy who had despoiled them, but they also felt themselves lowered by the incontestable superiority of his policy. It did no good to make Napoleon III responsible, for few were those, like Thiers, who had opposed him. Public opinion in general had shown sympathy for the emperor and had not criticized him until after his defeat. During the twenty years which elapsed between the war and his own fall, Bismarck dominated Europe. Although he did not appear to be bellicose, he lacked the skill to make his hegemony tolerable. Among his favorite instruments were threat and intimidation, and even when he sought merely to cause fear, evil intent could be attributed to him. Perhaps he himself was more prone to fear than has been supposed, and his famous remark about the "coalition nightmare" would seem to indicate that possibility.[42] He was not France's enemy, either on principle or through feeling. "France," he wrote to General Leopold von Gerlach, "interests me only to the extent to which she reacts to the situation of my own country . . . My attitude in respect to foreign governments does not stem from any immutable antipathies, but solely from the harmfulness or usefulness of those governments to Prussia . . . Isn't it more reasonable to be on good terms rather than bad with the French, as long as they leave us in peace?"

Those lines written to a close friend in 1857, and consequently anterior to the period of tension with France, before Bismarck had become prime minister, would seem to show that at that time he had no preconceived idea, no determined plan. In that case, the policy he evolved later was probably the result of circumstances arising in the ensuing years and was therefore not predestined. Although he yielded to the temptation to create German unity through war—a more striking and a quicker solution than others which appeared possible—did his opponents have to furnish him a pretext, by blocking an ineluctable phenomenon of history? The unification of Germany was not at all incompatible with an accord between the German and the French peoples. Was it necessary to rush into a military adventure for which he held all the trump cards, while France had none?

We may rightfully accuse Bismarck's mistrust of France after 1870, his opinion of the French as a people which had always been aggressive, and the alliances he concluded supposedly to protect himself against this people. The Frenchman of that time was no longer the Frenchman of the Napoleonic wars, and better attitudes toward him, with a frankly pacific policy, might have changed many things.

Yet France must be glad that Bismarck avoided the great alliance of the Germans with the Russians, which would have constituted a grave threat to her and to Europe. Hitler and Stalin would return to it.

[37] Hitler would find admirers and supporters among the French "fascists." Bismarck found none in any party.

[38] Forty years later, Bismarck would write: "I think that after the suppression of the revolt of March 19, 1848 (in Berlin), German unity could have been brought about in a stricter manner than it was later at the time I was part of the government." It is not very likely that the French government in 1848 would have opposed the crowning of the king of Prussia as emperor of Germany.

[39] On July 27, 1863, Bismarck had told the Prussian Chamber: "Since the life of states is not static, conflicts are transformed into questions of power, and the one which has it does as it pleases." A delegate, Count Schwerin, replied to this in his absence: "The sentence which was the climax of the prime minister's speech, 'Might makes right,' is not the

kind of statement on which the Prussian dynasty can take a stand." Bismarck always protested against this deformation of his words.

[40]This does not fully translate *staatsrechtlich*. Also involved here is a historic right, for the emperor of Vienna reigned for centuries over all Germany, and Bismarck's empire would constitute in reality a duplication of the former German Empire.

[41]Bismarck disliked having any general, however highly placed, encroach upon his powers, and he liked to say that diplomacy is more difficult than the military profession.

Lack of taste for the military profession was a family tradition. His father, a cavalry captain, had resigned his service duties at twenty-three; the king of Prussia deprived him of his commission and the right to wear the uniform; this right was restored later, but he did not take part in the Battle of Jena nor in the campaigns of 1812–1815 against Napoleon.

At the same age at which his father had left the service, Bismarck, with his father's approval, did all in his power to escape service. He wrote to his father: "A final attempt to get myself reclassified in Berlin has just failed. They have given me some hope of being released quickly because of a muscular weakness I said I had under my right arm when I raise it, supposedly the result of some blow."

In reality, young Bismarck was of athletic build, was an excellent horseman and swimmer. He was assigned to the cavalry of the guard, but was never in combat, since no war occurred during his youth.

[42]Just before the Berlin Congress, the Russian minister Shuválov reportedly said to Bismarck: "You are having the coalition nightmare," to which Bismarck replied, "Precisely." (*Pensées et Souvenirs*)

CHAPTER 9

The Dangerous Alliances

IN the period from 1870 to 1914, Franco–German relations seem to have a fatalistic character. This fatal aspect may be merely apparent, or perhaps even artificial. It is based on the idea that each of the two peoples formed of the other: the idea of the implacable enemy. Bismarck's entire policy was based on the hypothesis that France was thinking only of revenge. The French people never wanted a war of revenge, but there were more or less numerous, more or less influential individuals who did. Their loud claims were enough to worry the Germans, and to furnish the pretext for their policy.

And the Germans for their part furnished enough fuel to feed the flames of French uneasiness. Demographic and economic growth,[43] combined with military might, soon made Germany greater than France in all sectors. The wilfully provocative tone of many Germans and of the new emperor was hardly reassuring. Where William I had been reserved and modest, William II, a blunderer and a braggart, went on with his empty gestures and childish threats to disturb and harass not only the French but also a large part of the rest of the world. People no doubt took him too seriously. This military man spent twenty-seven years without going to war; he was fundamentally good-natured and hoped for a rapprochement with France. Nevertheless, mass populations, newspaper readers, even statesmen, cannot be expected to judge a ruler other than by his appearance. With William II, the destinies of Germany fell into the hands of a man who was the opposite of Bismarck, a man dangerous in his own way, although for different reasons. He was a boaster, inconsistent and impulsive, whose actions were unpredictable. His adversaries might have given some heed to the fact that his policy, a disastrous one for his country, was destroying Bismarck's work. He denounced the Reinsurance Treaty with Russia, which to a certain extent counterbalanced the Austrian alliance, and in so doing he made the Franco–Russian alliance inevitable. More than once he refused to make an alliance with England, driving her toward France.

This last fact, less well known than it should be, is worth emphasizing. As early as two years before his retirement, Bismarck had sent his proposals for an alliance to London; they were rather surprising proposals, and they remained unanswered.[44] In 1895, it was Prime Minister Salisbury who made overtures to Germany which were rejected by the Kaiser. In 1898 and 1899 they were resumed by Chamberlain, the minister for the colonies, who declared in a speech at Leicester, which stimulated world-wide interest: "Disraeli had long hoped that we should not remain isolated on the continent. I think that the most natural alliance would be an alliance with the German Empire. An entente between the two great nations would insure the peace of the world." In January, 1901, there occurred a new British attempt followed by a new failure.

It might seem astonishing to us that such offers were not given serious attention, if we forgot that William II had conceived the idea of vying with England for the mastery of the seas. A saying of his, "our future is on the water," explains his world policy *(Weltpolitik)* which he intended to set against the Bismarckian continental policy, or rather to have succeed it. His great adviser, Admiral von Tirpitz, led him to carry out ever vaster naval programs, which made any rapprochement with Great Britain impossible. The latter had to conclude the Entente Cordiale with France in 1904.

Is this serious error by the Kaiser imputable to him alone and the influence of the "Great Admiral"? It appears irrefutable that the Kaiser found support in a portion of German public opinion, in such associations as the Naval League or the Pan-Germanist League, and even in such enlightened men as Chancellor von Bülow, who stated his arguments for the imperial policy in his *Deutsche Politik*. He declared that Germany had to have a powerful navy to protect its foreign trade now grown to be quite important. Although the German fleet was second in the world in 1914, it was still quite inferior to the combined British, French, and Russian fleets; as a result, it was useless except for submarine warfare.

France and Germany

At a late date, Germany had won a colonial empire which was not of the first magnitude but which nevertheless had value. Her "world" policy might have been confined to exploiting this empire, and to developing her foreign trade, which was growing faster than her population. Between 1900 and 1913, Germany's exports had risen from 4,612 million marks to 10,097 million marks, and its population from 56 to 66 million. If it went beyond the twofold task of protecting the colonial empire and exploiting trade, the *Weltpolitik* would become merely empty manifestations, meaningless but dangerous formulae: *Drang nach Osten* (the drive to the East), at a time when Turkey was Germany's friend and when the Arabs, whom the Kaiser harangued at Damascus, still belonged to the Ottoman Empire; "living space," when Germany was living without any difficulties inside its borders; "our future is on the water," etc. Because of his incessant restlessness and his travels, his speeches made without rhyme or reason, and his saber rattling, the Kaiser finally came to be thought of as a sovereign thirsty for conquest, when in reality he was primarily having a good time parading about. This mania for showing off everywhere, for getting into quarrels, even over minor interests, which is characteristic of the Kaiser's policy, led Germany into conflict with France over Morocco. It would lead to a German defeat, since she found herself abandoned by Italy, with France supported by England. This dispute served as a test of the new alignment of powers resulting from the Entente Cordiale. Germany and her allies, or more accurately, her only ally, Austria–Hungary (since Italy was no longer anything but a *pro forma* member of the Triple Alliance) would henceforth be inferior to the opposing coalition.[45] It was then that the Kaiser and his subjects would be afflicted with the encirclement complex.

Even a cursory glance at the map shows that Germany, located at Europe's center, was running the risk of being surrounded. That is the great risk inherent in its geographical position, and its policy must be directed toward avoiding the danger. Bismarck had understood this, when he concluded the Reinsurance Treaty with Russia, which guaranteed his eastern border. He tried unsuccessfully to protect himself on the west by turning toward England. William II, after having rejected the Russian guaranty, had the unique opportunity of seeing the British alliance proposed to him; yet he repulsed Great Britain as he had repulsed Russia. How then can one talk of a wilful encirclement of Germany by her enemies? When she was at the very peak of her power, two great empires had seen her as a desirable partner, and had extended their hand to her. Either would have sufficed to insure her an unshakeable position. By refusing their friendship, Germany probably took the fatal step of making them her enemies.[46]

As for France, she did not come first in William's policy. Even though, while intervening everywhere, he clashed with her in Morocco, his attention was not particularly directed toward her. His "world" policy made it inevitable that he would encounter on his path the two great world powers, which were then England and Russia. Because he had been unable to come to an understanding with them, he would have to quarrel with the former over the fleet and with the latter over the Balkans.

He made feeble attempts at rapprochement with France, but they had no results. The conditions for an entente did not exist then in France or in Germany. France would have exacted major concessions concerning Alsace–Lorraine, and for Germany, these were not open to discussion. The dispute could be settled only by war or by a prolongation of peace which would, in the long run, have resulted in toleration of the *fait accompli*.

If we admit that the "cold war" between Germany and France was inevitable after 1870, in view of the feelings of the two peoples and their leaders, we must also grant that the French statesmen and diplomats played their game much better than the Germans—they were able to profit from William II's mistakes, and to return to alliances they had once scorned. We may still wonder, however, if these alliances, once they had insured the western camp's superiority over the central empires, might not have been used to negotiate a peaceful agreement. It has not been proved that Germany, no longer feeling she was the stronger, would have rejected it. Contrary to what has commonly been said, the feeling which prevailed inside Germany in the last years before the war was not the desire for conquest, but rather a kind of uneasiness over the growing superiority of the adversary.

At the time, no desire for an entente appeared on either side. The Moroccan dispute ended in a more or less lame compromise, but it was at least a compromise. It showed that France and Germany, after a bitter quarrel and despite their fundamental hostility, opted for peace; but the Balkan wars, which would place Russia and Austria–Hungary rather than

Germany and France in the foreground, revealed the existence of a center of trouble which was dangerous in another way, and out of which world war was to come.

When the war broke out, William II placed the blame on England. He was no doubt feeling remorse at having remained deaf to her appeals. "She is achieving," he exclaimed, "the greatest success of the world policy she has tenaciously pursued, a policy which is purely anti-German. Edward VII, after death, is still stronger than I am, and I am alive." He forgot that by building fewer ships (as Lord Haldane had proposed to him before the war), he could have avoided this "purely anti-German policy."

One of the principal causes of the war can be seen in the fact that the Kaiser's character was ill-suited to that of his people and to Germany's situation. Germany, after a late unification and a number of great victories in all fields, due partially to the exceptional Bismarck, had made a rapid rise. Was she to bend her strength to new military successes, or merely toward the development of her production and her wealth? The temptation to use her arms, if only as a means of putting pressure on other peoples, was great. William II was trying to concentrate on a dangerous game—as, for example, in the Moroccan affair. The game had the effect of coalescing the great European powers against him.

No German government could fail to take into account Germany's expansive force. Her growth was too recent for her not to be exceedingly aware of it. At the time, this people should have been guided by a calm, prudent man, who would have avoided any disturbing word or gesture, and who would have turned his mind toward reducing tensions in Germany's contacts with other peoples, while maintaining his country's place on the world chessboard. The task required a more humane Bismarck, less burdened with feudal heredity. But the Kaiser, with his impulsive nature, his restlessness, his provocative speeches, and lack of firmness in his plans, was the man least suited to lead this dynamic people, this Germany already given to being led astray. She needed less the iron fist that an adroit and sure hand on the reins; William II had neither, and he stumbled into catastrophe exclaiming, no doubt sincerely, that he had not desired it.

The war of 1914–1918 was not a Franco–German war, but an Austro–Russian one, into which France and Germany were drawn by their allies, Russia and Austria–Hungary. The fact that the major military operations took place in France does not alter the origins of the conflict.

On both sides, propaganda has obscured the causes of the war, but they are clearly revealed in the documents which have since been published, and in the works of impartial historians in most of the countries involved. Since these documents and histories are still unknown to the public at large, many people still are convinced that the Kaiser wanted to rule the world, or that the Allies wanted to annihilate Germany; these are all childish views which do not stand up under even a superficial critical examination. A people of sixty-six million inhabitants, as Germany was then, could not dominate the earth's two billion inhabitants. At the same time, this people could not be destroyed. It is true that the war did destroy the Austro–Hungarian Empire, but this was only a mosaic of different peoples, and its division had long been discussed by diplomats and in the press.

There is a generally accepted thesis that no one wanted this war, but that everyone, as the English expression goes, "muddled through"—all the nations got enmeshed in it, let themselves be drawn in through unwise actions or through negligence; in other words, there were all sorts of sins of commission and sins of omission. This thesis saves everyone's self-respect and certainly simplifies matters. It draws no distinction between the murder of Archduke Francis Ferdinand and the Austro–Hungarian reaction, or among the Russian, Austrian, and German mobilizations, or between the apparent inertia of France and the hesitancy of England—gestures and attitudes which possibly do not all have equal importance.

What must first be stressed is the atmosphere which had prepared this war. Europe was divided into two camps which in the preceding years, had become increasingly hostile. The great powers, without taking part in the two Balkan wars, had automatically aligned themselves behind the small powers, some on one side, some on the other—as if France, England, Germany, or Italy had any interest at all in whether a given little piece of ground became Serbian or Bulgarian, Albanian or Roumanian; certainly all these choices were absurd. Modern wars, in which the lives of millions of men and immense fortunes are at stake, should not be started—if one admits that they should be started at all—except for the most serious reasons. It is indeed illogical that half a dozen great powers should have been able to kill and destroy one another for over four years for a handful of little Balkan nations. Had these powers been reasonable, instead of trying to extend their influence over one or the other of the Balkan states, they would have drawn a line to isolate this malefic peninsula and to abandon these populations to their own internal struggles.

It can be maintained, it is true, that the Serbian affair was merely a pretext chosen hypocritically by the two blocs in order to go to war; that this war was in the air, but that no one dared take responsibility for declaring it. In view of the climate which was prevalent in Europe, one may also compare the whole continent to a pile of inflammable materials which any spark might have touched off. Yet those who were alive in those times remember that before the month of June, 1914, war was not in the air. There was a certain tension among the great powers, a tension which had increased because of the Balkan wars, but France and Germany, who had quarreled over Morocco without coming to blows, were not thinking of fighting over Belgrade. France had enough to do in her recently expanded empire. William II, who had not taken advantage of the weakening of Russia following her war with Japan, knew that the Russian army had since recovered, and the French army as well. As we have said, the Triple Entente represented a coalition which was superior to Germany with Austria–Hungary at her side. Why would the Kaiser throw his country into this struggle on two fronts, a struggle he had always feared? Except perhaps in the view of the German general staff[47] there were strong reasons for not desiring war either in Paris or Berlin. Was the situation the same in Vienna and Petersburg?

There it was a situation of two major powers engaged against each other by vital interests, not only because of their rivalry in the Balkans, which was growing more acute from year to year, but also because of the Slavic populations of the Austro–Hungarian Empire, who were being subjected to the pressures of Pan-Slavism and who were threatening to split apart the twofold monarchy. Threatened from within and from without, Austria–Hungary did not ask itself, or more precisely, its rulers did not ask, whether liberal and daring reforms might not better have insured the empire's security than an attack against a small neighboring state. As for czarist Russia, at least in its warlike, Pan-Slavist elements, it was only awaiting the opportunity to move to an attack on Austria–Hungary, with the support of the allies it had been successful in obtaining.

The mistake of France and Germany was forgetting that they had chosen dangerous allies, Russia on the one hand, Austria–Hungary on the other. In any alliance, not only the eventual aid must be weighed, but the risks as well, and the risks for France and Germany were far greater than for Russia and Austria–Hungary. The properly Franco–German quarrel, Alsace–Lorraine, had provoked no conflict since 1870. It belonged to the past, and its importance was diminishing from day to day. There was little likelihood that Russia would be involved in war over Alsace–Lorraine. Austro–Russian opposition in the Balkans and in the Danube basin belonged, however, to the present, and even more to the future; there was no common measure between the two allies, Russia and France; on the one side, small risks were growing ever smaller, on the other, big risks were getting bigger.

77

One wonders if the alliance was perhaps not taken seriously, and that possibility makes certain observations necessary. In the years preceding the war, France had placed herself more and more at the disposition of Russia. As early as 1899, the purely defensive nature of the alliance was modified by the introduction of the "balance" factor, which dangerously widened its scope. Russian policy, which had moved to the offensive in the Balkans, would not long delay in threatening this balance which France had pledged herself to maintain at Russia's side. France had given her word to an ally who was more dynamic and more enterprising, and who would involve her in adventures. France promised, in fact, to support Russia in her quarrels with Austria, and Austria had received similar assurances from Germany.

Opposition arose in France at the time to this new interpretation of the alliance. In 1909, Pichon, the minister for foreign affairs, refused support in the quarrel over Bosnia between Russia and Austria–Hungary. Hanotaux, the former minister for foreign affairs, writing in *Le Figaro*, said: "Of what concern is it to our French peasants whether Bosnia–Herzegovina is occupied or annexed?" Léon Blum asserted that the *casus foederis* did not exist in conflicts arising from Balkan disturbances and revolutions, and we can read in the correspondence of Isvolski, one of the great artisans of the war: "Caillaux and Clémenceau would not have France intervene in a Balkan conflict."[48] We can only observe that neither of these two Frenchmen was in power in 1914, and that those who were did little or nothing to restrain Russia. Had it been intimated to her that France would not accept war over an

Austro–Serbian quarrel, perhaps the Russian leaders would have been led to do some second thinking. The Germans should have acted the same way in reference to Austria.

In order to understand the actions and the abstentions of both groups, the failure of all diplomatic undertakings and the absence of other undertakings which might have succeeded we should have to discuss the whole problem of alliances. Alliances cannot be useful for preventing war unless they are conditional, unless each power agrees to supports its ally up to a certain point and then no further. To place oneself without reservation at the disposition of an ally, to underwrite in advance any policy it may please him to follow, is to encourage aggression and to run headlong into war.[49] Unfortunately, that is what Germany and France did in 1914, by tying themselves to Austria and to Russia. After having refused for forty-three years to go to war over Alsace–Lorraine, a matter much closer to them, they finally went to war over Serbia, which meant nothing to them.[50]

[43]In 1871, Germany, with 41 million inhabitants, had barely passed France. In 1914, France had 39 million, Germany 68 million.

[44]Bismarck, who said he had neither sympathy nor antipathy for any foreign nation, admitted nevertheless that he had never had any sympathy in his whole life except "for England and its people."

[45]Germany and Austria–Hungary, 120 million inhabitants; France–Russia, 240 million.

[46]We have to simplify things in this rapid review which is not intended to be a history textbook. In fact, William II did not deliberately and definitively reject the Russian alliance when he denounced Bismarck's Reinsurance Treaty. He tried to approach Russia several times. In 1897, he came

to an understanding with her in the China affair, against Japan, forcing Japan to give up Port Arthur. In return, Russia obtained Kiaochow for him. In 1904, when Russia was at war with Japan, he provided coal for her fleet. Far from thinking about taking advantage of her defeat in order to attack her, he met the czar at Björkö, concluding with him a defensive alliance to which he thought of joining France, already Russia's ally. Nicholas II's ministers had him annul this treaty, and it was not approved by the German Chancellor von Bülow. Exaggerating in his own mind his influence over his more reserved and timid cousin, he thought right up to the last minute that he could avoid war with Russia. Just before war broke out, he was still corresponding with Nicholas.

In reference to England, instances of vacillation can be seen, but there were also desires for rapprochement, less well defined, however, than his wishes for rapprochement with Russia. In 1890, Germany recovered the island of Heligoland, exchanged with England for Zanzibar. In 1899, after Chamberlain's offer of alliance, William II reversed his policy on the Boers whose side he had supported against Great Britain. In 1912, when Chancellor Bethmann–Hollweg favored an alliance with England, it appeared for a time as if the Haldane mission to Berlin on naval agreement would succeed.

All in all, it was not because of any desire to isolate himself that William II failed to obtain the alliances which were offered him; it seems rather that it was because of inconsistency, awkwardness, and even pride. He would refuse alliances when the time seemed right for them and pursue them when it had slipped by, with the possible partner having become involved elsewhere.

[47]There is little doubt that General von Moltke, chief of the general staff, whose conduct of the war would appear so mediocre, exercised strong pressure in favor of mobilization, and particularly at the last minute. As early as 1913 he said to the Bavarian minister in Berlin that "the moment seemed so favorable to him from the military point of view that according to all forecasts another one like it would not occur." In 1906, his predecessor, General von Schlieffen, had

wanted to take advantage of even more favorable circumstances to make preventive war on France. At that time, just after the Russo–Japanese War, the Russian chief of staff was telling his French counterpart that because of lack of *cadres* and *matériel*, his troops would be unable to carry out active operations for a year and a half.

One cannot but agree that if William II were really a warmonger, he missed a golden opportunity. He had listened neither to Schlieffen in 1906 nor to Moltke in 1913. However, a change must have occurred in his thinking if it is true that in November, 1913, he told the king of the Belgians that the fight with France seemed inevitable to him. Let us not forget, however, that remarks by the Kaiser, who spoke without thinking and whose inconsistency is well known, must always be taken cautiously.

[48]Ribot, however, was saying as early as 1892: "It would not be in our interest to maintain neutrality in the case of an Austro–Russian conflict." Ambassador Saint Aulaire would later write that from 1912 on, French policy sought to "feed the Franco–Russian alliance on the Austro–Russian rivalry."

[48]Excellent historians, among them Pierre Renouvin, assert that "the French government was obliged to take into account Russia's interest or be guilty of violating the alliance." But taking an ally's interests into account doesn't mean that you will support her completely, unconditionally, and that you will identify yourself with her. This theory was to lead France into two world wars, the first to support Russia, the second to defend Poland, and without Russia's or Poland's gaining any advantage from it.

What can be said of France and Russia would also apply to Germany and Austria–Hungary. A German diplomat who was quite involved in the events, M. von Tschirsky, ambassador to Vienna, wrote shortly before the war: "How many times have I not asked myself if it was worth the cost to bind ourselves so firmly to this collection of states which is cracking in every direction."

During the 1914 crisis, only Italy was able to free herself in time, when she understood that the interests of her allies were not her interests.

[50]Historians of various nationalities have shown in detail the negotiations which preceded the opening of hostili-

ties. What comes out of all this is primarily that Russia drove toward war, that the peace-loving czar could not restrain the zeal of his ministers and general staff, and that on the French and British side, little was done to restrain those on corresponding levels. The Russian mobilization was decreed on July 30, and the governments and the military leaders admitted that it started the war automatically. War was declared by Germany on Russia on August 1, and on France August 3; England declared war on Germany on August 4. The British government had made four proposals for mediation or conference on July 24, 26, 27, and 29; it is not clear from these whether it did not want the war to start or did not want to get into it if it did start. The Kaiser apparently thought England wouldn't intervene and flew into a violent rage when he learned of the British declaration of war. He began by supporting Austria–Hungary to the hilt, and declared, after Serbia had accepted the Austrian ultimatum that all danger of war had been avoided. But then he rejected the British proposals. Austria, after demonstrating her intractability with Serbia, let it be known that she was ready to talk, but it was too late.

CHAPTER **10**

Versailles

THE Versailles Treaty brought an end to a war which had broken out in unhealthy conditions and for objectives which did not interest all the beligerents. For four years an effort had been made to hide this fact from the public, the Allies trying to make people think that the democracies (the czar's democracy, for example!) were fighting imperialism, while the Germans claimed that they were defending their territory and their people against destruction (by annexing, for example, Belgium and Poland). The best known barb about the treaty is that of Bainville: "too harsh in its mild elements, too mild in its harsh elements." A striking formula by a brilliant journalist, but it does not correspond to reality. If it had been possible to impose on Germany conditions harsher than those of Versailles—and in fact, it was impossible—such conditions would only have caused her to draw closer to Russia and to cement between the two great powers the alliance they had failed to obtain just before the war. It would have made them sooner or later the masters of Europe; it was not concluded, but would have been if the pressures of the treaty had been increased. Germany, fearing communism, was satisfied with mild gestures such as the treaties of Rapallo (1922) or of Berlin (1926). Much more serious was the Hitler–Stalin pact of 1939, although on the German side, it was merely a feint.

Even if defeated, two peoples as numerous, energetic, and dynamic as the Russians and the Germans could not be struck off the map of the world. In the years following the war, the Allies made a pretense of determining policy as if these two peoples did not exist, as if a cloud of little states had taken their places on the diplomatic chessboard. These little nations which claimed to be national states but which, in reality, were made up of bits and pieces like the Austria-Hungary from which they came, were to complicate European politics and finally to provoke a new war. National socialism and then communism would sweep them away.

Experience showed that the conquerors of Germany were incapable of making her respect their treaty. It is difficult to decide whether this means that the treaty was not applicable, or whether the victors applied it badly. Both possibilities may be true. There were serious faults in the way in which the treaty was conceived. In its application, however, such a broad treaty can always be rectified in such a way that its major points of difficulty are smoothed over and that it may become viable. The blunders of the Allies and the ill will of the Germans prevented this from being done. The initial difficulty was to bring into agreement all the contradictory views of the victors; many clauses of the treaty are merely compromises between these opposing views. The divergences were accentuated when people began to try to explain them. In the absence of any common policy, each of the victors established one of his own.

England and France have bitterly reproached each other for their respective attitudes. In France it is freely admitted that England was following a poor policy; but why should she have carried out a pro-France policy, if her own interests dictated another? If France and England had desired to maintain their alliance in peacetime, they should have worked together constantly and should have discussed problems and come to agreement before taking action; in short, they should have set a policy in reference to Germany. In that way, and only in that way, did they have any opportunity to impose their point of view. Each pulled in his own way, and although France sometimes yielded to England, it also happened that she would defend her views stubbornly, and even then she had to go it alone.

The formula "reparations and security" which dominated the drafting of the treaty, as legitimate as it may appear, was not above question. This twofold requirement ought to have been made subordinate to a third, which was more important, namely the necessity for a *modus vivendi* with Germany. No one thought of it. People might have said to each other that in the life of nations, hostility between neighbors is never eternal. The ease with which the age-old fight with England had been ended could have been used as an example. Two cruel wars with Germany in the space of a half-century were an indication. The first had brought up Alsace–Lorraine as the apple of discord, and the second had done away with it. Since France was recovering her lost provinces, nothing stood in the way of an agreement between the two countries. Agreement between two former enemies is reached only through a moderate peace, in which the victor limits his claims to the essentials. It should not have been forgotten either that in this war there were many victors, and that all of them except America had claims, the huge total of which meant that it would be difficult for the debtor to honor the bill.[51]

The question of a possible and necessary entente was not even raised. It was admitted a priori that there could be no understanding with Germany; the German people was a domineering, warmongering, dangerous people which had to be rendered harmless by multiple controls. The maximum must be exacted from it and it must be made incapable of doing harm. These premises were set forth as unquestionable, and the formula of "reparations and security" seemed to flow from them logically. We say "seemed," but things were really not so simple. Never has a victor obtained the impossible from the vanquished. One can name astronomical figures, hundreds of billions, and say that one has a right to such amounts, but that does not mean that the other side has the money in its pocket. You can prevent a great people from having soldiers—why not children, too?

Reparations

To begin with, was this term "reparations" well chosen? In fact, the sums asked of Germany were to be used to pay for war damage, but why talk of "reparations" rather than "indemnities" as was customary? It's always the conquered nation who pays, not because it has caused the damage, but because it has lost the war. Had France been defeated, not only would she have incurred reparations payments, but she also would have had to pay a tribute to Germany, even though, since she was the major theater of operations, she had suffered all the damage. That was what had happened in 1871.

The word "reparations" implies that it is a matter of something due, since Germany was responsible for the war. Why should the idea of responsibility be brought in at this point, since, as everyone knows, it is the fact of being the victor which allows one to obtain an indemnity, and not that of having suffered damage or of having started the war? In the preceding chapter we saw that the problem of the various responsibilities was extremely complex in the war of 1914–1918. Most of the belligerents came to understand this. It was up to the historians and posterity to try to solve it; it could not be taken up in the peace treaty without irritating the defeated side to no purpose, without incurring its ill will.

The substitution of reparations for the traditional war indemnity involved immediate and dangerous consequences. The amount of an indemnity is set once and for all, immediately and finally by the conqueror according to what he thinks he can obtain from the conquered. The minute it becomes a matter of reparations, the damage to be repaired must be assessed—a most difficult, if not impossible task. It goes without saying that the estimate of the payer is very far from that of the payee, and that the establishment of a sum for "repairs" gives rise to endless controversy. That is one of the causes which contributed to the reparations fiasco.

In 1871, Bismarck had asked for five billion francs, the equivalent of four billion marks. Twenty to thirty billion marks might have been asked, by relating payments to the progressive evacuation of the occupied territories. This method is probably not the only possible one, but its results are certain. It could not fail with Germany, since she would have hastened to pay in order to free her territories. Seeing astronomical figures proposed to them—at first it was one hundred thirty-two billion marks in gold—the Germans turned a deaf ear. At Versailles, Brockdorff–Rantzau's proposal that this sum be reduced to one hundred billion was indignantly rejected. The Dawes Plan set the sum at one and a half to two and a half billions per year, but without specifying the number of annual payments. The Young Plan reduced the figure, but spread the payments over sixty years, as if any debtor had ever paid over so long a period!

The estimates being as unrealistic as they were variable, the Germans told themselves that they had nothing to do but wait, and that their debt would disappear by itself. And that is what happened. As early as 1932, less than fourteen years after the end of the war, Germany stopped all payments, with the consent of her creditors, who gave up perhaps a bit quickly.

Aside from the Bismarck method, there were other excellent means of obtaining payment—reparations in kind, according to the Loucheur–Rathenau Plan, for example. It had been tried. The German government could no longer say that it lacked foreign exchange, since deliveries would be made by its manufacturers whom it paid in marks. But the French industrialists saw competition in this mode of reparations, although reparations could have been planned without harming them. If one thinks of France's needs and of her empire's needs in terms of equipment (canals, highways, hydroelectric plants, etc.), needs which French industry could not meet, one must admit that the labor and the productive capacity of Germany could have been utilized without harming anyone at all.

An empty discussion went on over her capacity to pay; some—the Englishman Keynes, for example—asserted that it was overestimated while others maintained the opposite view. Strictly speaking, the capacity of a people to pay cannot be defined. It is a highly relative concept, varying according to the work and the sacrifices people impose on themselves, and those which others may wish to impose on them, or be able to impose. If one is in a position to establish controls over a nation's work, to force it to tighten its belt for ten years and more, then its payment potential may be high. If one does not do that, the potential is perforce limited by the people's good will, which may be in short supply. In other words, only constraint, and rather drastic constraint, could draw substantial payments from a people like the Germans.

89

France and Germany

The Soviets would understand that after World War II. Occupying only a third of the German territory, they obtained, in less than ten years, reparations estimated to be higher than those the other Allies received after 1918. The Russians took all of the economy of their zone into their own hands, and the German population endured severe privation. The Russians thus gave Westerners a "lesson in reparations"; if we didn't want to do things this way, it was useless to complain about German ill will.[52]

Right of peoples

Although reparations poisoned the Franco–German atmosphere, territorial problems take first place after a major conflict. They are the most important because they determine future wars. For France, these territorial questions were easily settled: she recovered Alsace–Lorraine. The issue of the left bank of the Rhine did come up but it was quickly set aside; the old French patriot, Clémenceau, did not want to annex Germans, nor did most of the French population for that matter. Nevertheless, the changes made in Europe were considerable and they could not remain without influence on French policy and on Franco–German relations. The victors intended to reshape Europe according to the right of peoples to self-determination, which President Wilson took from the French Revolution. Many objections may be made to this principle, yet it would be acceptable if it were really applied, after having been carefully defined.

Exactly what was being called a "people" was never stated. The principle is being applied at random today to peoples in Africa and elsewhere who had no existence as peoples yesterday. Their lines of demarcation come from former colonies whose boundaries were fixed by chance, and which generally included different tribes. Someday there will be further discussion about these states which have been improvised according to a principle. The prognosis remains doubtful.

According to this theory, the right of peoples to self-determination must be translated by referendums, and these may result in embarrassing cases. Suppose that a people decides by a low majority—fifty-two per cent, for example, in favor of such and such a status—by opting for the majority, they will consequently be violating the rights of forty-eight per cent of the population. Can it be said that it has determined itself, or that the majority determined the minority? Let us note that this is an entirely different case from those votes which regularly occur in a democracy on minor questions and which can be annulled by a later vote; this is a matter of the fate and the future of a people—can it be decided by a process as delicate as that of universal suffrage? Indeed, voting implies change; all voters are changeable. The Saar, called upon several times to choose between France and Germany, decided for one at one time, for the other at another time. In the last vote, it chose for Germany. We are right in admitting that this vote is the definitive one, since the people of the Saar are German, but one wonders if it was ultimately their vote which decided their status as Germans; everyone already accepted that status, and it could have been recognized without the vote, just as the status of the Rhinelanders, the Würtembergers, or the Bavarians had been.

91

France and Germany

After World War I, the right of peoples was applied particularly to the Austro–Hungarian Empire which it had destroyed. In addition to a German minority, this empire included Hungarians, Czechs, Poles, Yugoslavs, Roumanians, and Italians, and many preferred to join a national state rather than belong to a conglomeration of peoples. However, the old Hapsburg Empire could have been modernized and transformed into a federation; a powerful, well-balanced state might have been made of it, capable of maintaining its place in Europe, whereas its weak successors were unable to maintain their independence. Even if we rule out that possibility, the experiment which was attempted could have been successful if the new Czech state had included only Czechs, the Polish state only Poles, and so on—in other words, if there had been truly national states, as people claimed to be creating, and not mixtures of peoples, Austria–Hungary in miniature. Giving to a Czechoslovakia of 13,600,000 inhabitants 3,300,000 Germans, 800,000 Hungarians, 400,000 Ukranians, and 100,000 Poles, to say nothing of 2,500,000 Slovaks who were assimilated into the 6,500,000 Czechs with whom they never got along; establishing Poland with thirty per cent of its population formed by groups of other races, and Roumania with twenty-five per cent, was all tantamount to condemning the new states in advance. An old nation like France could not absorb a foreign element of ten per cent; it is not clear how the small nations, with a much lower power of assimilation, could take care of much stronger national minorities.

The overworked argument that satisfactory boundaries could not be drawn because the populations were mixed was not valid. They were not mixed everywhere (the Sudeten Germans, for example, formed a bloc), and where they were, a part might have been transferred so as to obtain homogenous groupings, or things arranged so that in two neighboring countries with mixed populations there would be equivalent minorities.[53]

The result of this ineffective division was to multiply territorial claims among the small nations. Hungary never agreed to having Hungarians taken from her to be handed over to her neighbors. In 1939, after Munich, the Poles would take the Teschen district from the numerically inferior Czechs. This kind of situation became more threatening if the nation which considered itself the injured party was a great power. It was impossible to believe that Germany would continue to accept the fact that three million Sudeten Germans, living all along its boundary, were under Czech control. In order for Czechs and Sudetens to go on living together, what was required was not for some to be controlled by others, but to have a regime in which each nationality would have the same rights. The nationalism of the newly formed little states did not permit it.

The fate of the new states of Central and Eastern Europe mattered little to French policy if France did not choose to support them and to make allies of them against Germany. All France and her big allies had to do was not to yield to the childish imperialism of these newborns, and to deny them foreign populations to which they had no rights. An exclusively Czech Czechoslovakia, with its three million Germans removed, would have been stronger than a Czechoslovakia encumbered by non-Czech populations which she could not assimilate. Reduced to her own nationals, she might have lived without giving offense to anyone. Like Poland or Roumania, she would have been a natural friend for France, but, loaded with explosive elements which sooner or later would insure Germany's hostility to her, she became an ally for France against Germany, an ally destined to replace Russia; a fly in the place of an elephant, a superfluous and dangerous ally.

The Corridor

Poland's case was different. More important than Czechoslovakia, but badly located, she turned both Germany and Russia against her, the latter when she took over four million white Russians and Ukranians, the former because of the Danzig Corridor. The Poles, a brave but rash, imprudent people, did not hesitate, as soon as their state had been ressuscitated, to find motives for quarreling at the same time with both of their big neighbors, who had been oppressing them for over a century. In this case, France and her allies were not innocent. Although Poland alone was responsible for extending her territory eastward after the Versailles Treaty, the famous corridor, of which Foch said that it would start the next war, was the handiwork of France, England, and America. Economists asserted that Poland could not do without access to the sea; historians said that the corridor had already existed in the eighteenth century; yet Switzerland, Czecholslovakia, Austria, and Hungary did not have access to the sea either, and the small Prussia of Frederick was not yet big Germany.

We live in the twentieth century, not in the eighteenth, and what may have been acceptable then is much less acceptable now. There was no public press, or radios, railroads, automobiles, compulsory education; people moved about little, and since one could, after all, go by boat from Königsberg to Stettin, it mattered little if the Danzig Corridor lay between. East Prussia, in relation to the rest of Prussia, was like Ireland in relation to England, but it was an island separated from the mainland by a tongue of land instead of an arm of the sea. Modern technocracy changes everything. Newspapers showed millions of Germans the map of mutilated Germany, and the map was displayed to millions of school children; millions of drivers had to cross two boundaries to cross the corridor. On the trains, cars had to be sealed to avoid customs inspections. Out of this all too visible division between the two parts of Germany, out of this constraint highlighted by many forms of propaganda, a suggestion would be born, and would become a popular obsession. All Germans had to say, "Our country has undergone an unbearable mutilation, and we must put an end to it." It was certainly not so unbearable that it kept them from conducting business for twenty years. Means could have been found to simplify passage through the corridor; this had been discussed. The German people, however, would find themselves unable to resist when a daredevil like Hitler would say to them: "Follow me, we're going to do away with it."[54]

Marshal Pilsudski is said not to have been in favor of the Danzig Corridor. A soldier before he became the head of a government, he may perhaps have seen the danger better than did the politicians. The corridor could not be held in time of war; in 1939, it would fall into German hands in forty-eight hours. All we can do is deplore the statesmen's lack of imagination; if they wanted to give Poland access to the sea, they could have found a solution other than the splitting of Germany into two parts. This split, never accepted by the Germans, sentenced France to a new war with Germany if she allied herself with Poland; such an alliance, since it hardened the Polish position, prevented any amiable settlement of the corridor problem, a settlement which might someday have been found to modify the treaty.

This treaty being what it was—subject to criticism, but also subject to revision, like any other treaty—it was certainly the height of superficiality and blindness to pledge oneself to go to war in order to maintain one of its most serious errors.

Disarmament

We shall not dwell on other provisions of the Treaty of Versailles which would prove ineffectual. Disarming a great people is a completely vain hope; it can be controlled only in the early years, when this people, mentally and physically exhausted, has no desire to rearm.[55] When it grows strong again, all control becomes impossible. The Allies also committed the error of offering German disarmament as a simple, initial step toward general disarmament which would be attained in a few years; it never occurred. Could nations disarm when none knew the status of Soviet armament? Hitler, however, would not understand things that way. Since the others refused to take a position according to the disarmament of

Germany, he decided that Germany could take her position according to the disarmament of the others.

The strategic precautions taken in the name of "security" were equally vain. Following Prussia's example—her generals asserted in 1870 that the Metz forts were worth 10,000 men—it was believed that the strategic frontier of France should be taken to the Rhine, which was tantamount to the demilitarization of the left bank. A fortified city, a wide river, and a mountain chain had not been without value in the past, although Hannibal crossed the Alps with elephants and Napoleon without them. The Rhine, moreover, had never stopped the invasions of the Celts, Germans, Huns, and so on— nor in the opposite direction, the incursions of the Romans into Germany nor those of Louis XIV or the revolutionary armies. Without a German garrison, the left bank of the Rhine became a no man's land into which, in case of war, French troops could march easily and without risk, unless the Germans moved first. The speed of modern transport makes such precautions useless; a zone of this kind is crossed in two hours by motorized divisions, in a few minutes by planes carrying parachutists and bombs. Today, the only possible defense would be vast territories like those of Russia or the deserts of Africa, where large armies could maneuver, but where transportation facilities consume huge quantities of dwindling stocks of gasoline. Small countries, among which France and Germany must be classed henceforth, can no longer play the role of buffer zones. It goes without saying that atomic weapons now cancel all security considerations on which one could rely in 1919 or 1939.

France and Germany

Alliances

We wonder if the problem of alliances was better solved by France, who saw herself abandoned by her former allies. This fact caused bitter reflexion in France—as if England had any obligations toward France! A country makes or breaks its alliances according to what it judges its interest to be. England's interest was not bound up in ours, and the only thing to do, which no government sought to do, was to harmonize the interests of the two peoples. In less than a half-century, France had had two wars with Germany, and rightly or wrongly she saw the hereditary enemy in her. This was not the point of view of Great Britain or the United States, whose participation in the war had been rather fortuitous, and whose geographic location exposed them less than France to attack from a continental power. Neither had been at war with Germany before 1914, and about 1900, England had come close to being allied with her. With a little skill, the leaders of Germany easily could have obtained British and American neutrality.

When hostilities were over, with the German fleet sunk and her colonies confiscated, the English saw no further motives for opposing her. After all, the war had broken out over a Balkan conflict between Austria and Russia. The British tradition is to adapt to situations, to wait for them to take form, and to avoid long-term engagements. Austria no longer existed, and Russia was for the time being outside the main current of world politics. The situation of Europe was an entirely new one. Would Germany necessarily be tomorrow's enemy? Was it indispensable or urgently necessary to form a league against her? She had lost her army, and the only big army in Europe was that of France.

These facts are enough to explain England's attitude; she had gone to war of her own free will, out of fear of German domination, and if a new German threat should occur, she would again be at France's side.[56] Nevertheless, this did not mean that she would be ready to participate in any Franco–German war whatsoever or in no matter what coalition against Germany. The weak point in France's policy was that she had become involved in alliances with small nations, which she intended as replacements for the Russian alliance. In this way she was rushing forward over dangerous ground, promising to defend a new territorial status which was contested and contestable, and to support those nations in their eventual disputes with Germany. In short, she established herself as the guarantor of the Versailles boundary lines, something no other great power had done or was willing to do.

England did not and could not follow France along this path. She had accepted the creation of the new states, and the enlargement of certain others, but she didn't have absolute confidence in their future, and had no thought at all of fighting for the Polish Corridor, or to insure Czech domination over the Sudeten Germans. She was little interested in adopting these new allies against Germany; in her eyes, this would have amounted to creating a new anti-German front which would determine German policy in advance. England preferred to wait, to see how Germany would act; she thought that if the small nations were supported against Germany, they would be prevented from settling their differences with her, and that tension would be increased in Europe.

The future would show that all these ideas were both right and wrong. England saw herself obliged to aid Poland against Germany after having seen Czechoslovakia go under for lack of adequate help. France came to understand that her alliances had been useless; they saved neither Czechoslovakia nor Poland, and they contributed to touching off a new world war.

One can carry out only the policy of one's strength. Although France, in 1919 and the years which followed, thought she was capable of defending the Versailles boundary lines, even alone, she was no longer capable of it in 1939, in view of the rearming of Russia and Germany. As a matter of fact, France, just after Versailles, did not need alliances; she could be content with the Entente Cordiale, which had been tested and proved, and which in peacetime could have been more skillfully managed, giving more flexibility to her policy, and greater freedom of action. Thus with England, she could have played the role of mediator between Germany and the the small powers, without permitting the emergence of the kinds of dispute Hitler would solve by brute force, and without oscillating between the defense of untenable positions and capitulation to Germany.

[51]Considered simply as territory, the two provinces claimed by France, Alsace and Lorraine, represented 14,500 sq. km., but the total of the territories taken from Germany was more than 70,000 sq. km., the equivalent of eleven or twelve French departments—to say nothing of the German colonies, another three million sq. km.

[52]The allowance in kind taken from East Germany by the Soviets are estimated at 70 billion marks.

[53]For example, if there were a million Hungarians in Roumania, things could be arranged so that there would be a million Roumanians in Hungary, or they could be exchanged.

[54]Could Polish access to the sea not have been obtained by creating a Polish port on the Vistula, inland from the German coast, allowing the Polish flag to be flown on the high seas? Aren't most of the big European ports—Bremen, London, Amsterdam, Rotterdam, Antwerp, Rouen, Nantes, Bordeaux—river ports, sometimes sixty miles or more from the sea? Ships going to Antwerp have to go up the Escaut, through Dutch territory; the Belgians are not known to have complained. Polish vessels would have been in precisely the same situation if they went through German territory to reach the Baltic.

Poland could also reach the sea through Lithuania, a small country with which it had been united from the fourteenth to the eighteenth century. This union could have been re-established in the interest of both peoples, since the small nation of two million inhabitants had little chance of survival with three big neighbors. As things turned out, Lithuania did not survive and was absorbed by Russia.

[55]An example of this would be given after World War II by Germany herself, where the "count me out" party, favoring disarmament, opposed as strongly as it could the rearmament which Chancellor Adenauer had decided upon at the instigation of the Western powers.

[56]England was not attacked by Germany in 1914 nor in 1939. It was she who declared war, showing thereby that she did not shrink from decisions when her interest so dictated. But she would also feel completely free in respect to Germany. Before the war the Germans, for their part, had not really considered her an enemy. Their attacks on her were somewhat artificial. William II, although he vituperated his uncle Edward VII, always felt attracted to England, and his attitude was like that of the disappointed suitor.

This difference in the situation of the two adherents to the Entente Cordiale was basic. How could it be forgotten?

A Franco-German Episode

THE Weimar Republic, which replaced the defeated empire, was provided with a rather good constitution, but it had several defects which would prove fatal.[57] Although it did not lack men of good will, it had few real statesmen, with the exception of Stresemann, who died at fifty-one. Others, like Erzberger and Rathenau, who were the victims of assassins, merely appeared for a time in minor roles.

The new regime had to implement a difficult and highly unpopular treaty. By the very fact of its severity, however, the treaty offered possibilities to the victors as well as to the vanquished: what is written is not necessarily what is done, and a treaty is modified by conciliation or attrition. The Versailles Treaty would become a dead letter fifteen years later, but how did it come to that? The victors first showed intransigence, then changed to a policy of concessions which came too late, and finally gave up everything—reparations, limitation of German armament, demilitarization of the left bank of the Rhine. They even permitted Germany to take over vast territories, something conquerors never grant without war. As for the Germans, except for a brief period, they showed a total lack of flexibility, and finally the most brutal coolness. This method would succeed for them until it provoked a new disaster.

The fact which dominated the German scene in 1919 was the existence of a nationalist opposition, an important minority group, directed by short-sighted, stubborn men, with great financial means. This group did all it could to undermine the authority of the government, crying scandal every time the government showed any willingness to cooperate with the victors, and intimidating and arousing public opinion until the day when it would become the master of public opinion.

The Allies and the various democratic governments which succeeded each other in Germany up to 1930 were faced with the same difficulty: the problem was how to repress this nationalism which threatened the constitution and the treaty, to stifle its voice and to take away its arguments, which were based partly on errors and lies, but also on the policies of the victors. The German nationalists had not considered themselves defeated in 1918; they retained the illusion of impending victory right up to the armistice.[58] Wasn't the German army encamped all over Europe, and wasn't it in enemy territory when it capitulated? The peace treaty appeared not only as a bitter document for German self-respect, registering a new balance of forces to Germany's detriment, but also as an injustice, an imposture that had to be eliminated by whatever means possible.

The German people should have been reminded, through a well organized information campaign, that its nationalists were in error, that it had been defeated and must suffer the consequences, but also that the situation could be discussed; that once the treaty was signed, arrangements could be made. Here was a dialogue to be carried on with the two parts of the German people, a difficult, double dialogue, but it was indispensable. With a democratic regime, with a very young democracy not yet sure of itself, men of good will should have supported and helped to overcome their adversaries. There was, moreover, a policy to be followed with these adversaries if they came to power, a policy which it would have been well to determine in advance, and even to make known to the Germans. In that way they would have known what lay in store for them if they backed their madmen.

In short, the side of reasonable men should have been openly adopted, the side of men ready for conciliation, but whose good will should also have been rewarded with visible concessions. A collaboration had to be established, by which the application of the treaty would be constantly controlled by common accord. No one should have lost sight of certain conditions: (1) do not ask the impossible; (2) give the impression that what was asked would definitely be accomplished. If it had been said, for example, that after the payment of a stipulated sum, such and such a territory would be evacuated, another after the payment of another stipulated sum, then the Germans would have understood. But the evacuation schedules had been established in advance, and the sums exacted were such that the periods of time required to pay them were much too long. All guarantees had been dropped in order to obtain these payments.

Instead of giving the Germans the impression that they would gain by carrying out the treaty, the Allies managed to give them the impression that they would gain rather by not carrying it out. They did not make a sharp enough distinction between an incorrigible opposition party and a government which, although wanting to comply, could not do so always. They sometimes pretended to include all the Germans in the same reprobation, thus turning all of them against them. Instead of acting, the Allies grew indignant and protested; this had the effect of bearing out the views of the resistance element, that force of inertia which finally triumphed. "Why give satisfaction to the Allies up to a certain point, why pay them in a certain measure," argued the nationalists, "if it is possible for us to pay nothing?" Events proved them right. Their tactics won against the demands of the Allies, swept away the treaty, and the Weimar Republic along with it.

It is the conquerors who must be blamed first of all, for those who have the power have the essential responsibility in drafting and in implementing a treaty. The German republicans, on the other hand, often acted spinelessly and awkwardly. They too, inside their country, had the power and could dispose of power, had they known how, at the beginning of their regime, to forge an army devoted to them. They allowed the army to fall under their nationalistic opponents,

105

who revealed total absence of restraint in their politically senseless attacks. The nationalists saw neither the advantage that Germany could have by coming to agreement with the victors, nor the power of the National–Socialist wave which would finally wash over them. These old German nationalists, remnants of pre-war days, had conceived great ambitions and great hopes; they now considered themselves frustrated and they did not want to understand either the lesson of the defeat, nor the threat which Hitler and his fellow-travelers meant for them. The masses which the new man mobilized had nothing in common with the country gentlemen, the bourgeois, and the military men who had supported Pan–Germanism. They were above all the malcontents, the victims of war, inflation, and unemployment, a dough easily worked in the hands of a dictator who would force upon German policy a completely different style from that of Bismarck and William II. Men like Hindenburg, Hugenberg, Papen, ghosts of a decayed nationalism, would not carry much weight against the bold adventurers who would find their support in the lower classes, and no longer in the privileged classes.[59]

In order to follow Franco–German relations in the Weimar period, we must give particular attention to the Briand–Stresemann episode. Legend has it that Briand held out to Germany a hand which it rejected, and that he let himself be hoodwinked by his counterpart. It is true that Stresemann was more realistic; his position as minister of a conquered country required that it should be he, not his counterpart, who should ask for concessions. Urged on by home opinion, by implacable opponents, he was eager to obtain them.

Briand did little more to promise them. Later, either through negligence, or because French opinion did not support him, he reneged. He was criticized for the little he did cede. Wasn't this attempt at rapprochement based on a misunderstanding? In France, the majority wanted no understanding with Germany; what they expected of her was evidence of good will. In Germany, people were hoping for a relaxing of the Versailles Treaty; if these demands were not incompatible, tenacity and time would be required to reconcile them, and both ministers lacked time; Stresemann would die in 1929, Briand in 1932.

Their policy began with the Locarno Pact, under which Germany pledged not to change its western boundaries by war. It willingly recognized the demilitarization of the Rhineland imposed by Versailles. This transformation of an imposed condition into one which was freely accepted constituted but slight progress. As for the pledge not to change the boundary by war, it was tantamount to a non-aggression pact, and everyone knows how much such pacts are worth. Streseman had not promised the maintenance of the status quo, but merely maintenance of the peace, which did not exclude means other than war for modifying the status quo.[60]

The value of the treaty for France was based first of all on the warranty given by Italy, Belgium, and particularly, Great Britain; this was a means of obtaining the alliance which England had spurned up to that time. It was an alliance which was limited, moreover, to the case of German aggression on our eastern border, and it did not take into account the Franco–Polish nor the Franco–Czechoslovakian alliances.

Later the question of an "Eastern Locarno" did arise. Neither Germany nor England was eager to conclude it; for Germany it would have meant recognizing the Danzig Corridor, which no German could accept; England was unwilling to become embroiled in the conflicts of eastern Europe. France's security could not be assured by a Franco–Anglo–German treaty, at a time when France had already concluded alliances against Germany and when England refused to participate in them. There was consequently from the very first an insoluble contradiction in the Locarno attempt. It was certainly beyond the powers of Briand and Stresemann to have our boundaries guaranteed by Germany and to try to add the guarantee of the corridor for Poland. This addition was nevertheless indispensable if one wanted a complete and consistent securtiy system.[61]

Stresemann, who entertained no illusions about the full implication of the treaty, apparently saw in it a possible gesture toward France. He had taken the initiative here at the instigation of Lord d'Abernon, the ambassador from Great Britain to Berlin. Certainly this was one of those indications of good will that French opinion demanded. Although Briand, as a good Frenchman, had a weakness for pacts, it is far from certain that he saw anything more in this one.

In 1926, a year later, the Thoiry luncheon which marked the high point of the two statesmen's friendship, produced no results. Stresemann, sensing the rise of nationalist opposition, thought in the following years that he could fight it by asking for the evacuation of occupied territories; this required more time than he thought—it was not accomplished until 1930, a year after his death. "I have felt," he had said, "that I was the last bulwark of Germany against the fascist chaos. Yet we have been able to show the public no tangible success of our policy. The evacuation of the occupied territories will decide the fate of the Republic." He erred; when foreign troops did withdraw, success did not go to the parties that had obtained the concession, but to the Nazis, who now for the first time entered the Reichstag in strength. The fate of the Republic would indeed soon be settled, and without reference to the gift made to Germany of evacuation five years ahead of schedule. The gift may have come too late; but if we consider the events which followed, we might be tempted to think that the evacuation of the Rhineland was carried out too soon, since it took from the Allies their only remaining trump in the fight against German nationalism.

Stresemann had been called a nationalist. Isn't a statesman defending the interests of his country always more or less a nationalist? When his country is occupied, can he do less than ask for its liberation? Stresemann had endorsed the Young Plan; from the German point of view it raised many objections. Stresemann's own party denounced him and went on to demand a plebiscite against the plan. Later he would be reproached for the word *finassiren* found in his *Carnets*. Briand would have been the first to smile over it; who ever thought that trickery wasn't the very seat of diplomacy![62] The French, whose most famous diplomat had said, "Language was made to disguise thought," ought to have refrained from feigned indignation at this harmless slip.

The statements that both Briand and Stresemann are reported to have made show that these two men always had high regard for each other, and that they pursued sincerely their goal of France–German rapprochement. They were of quite a different turn of mind and of different character. The more positive Stresemann thought certain of Briand's ideas were inconsistent. When at Geneva Briand pushed the idea of the United States of Europe, Stresemann was somewhat reserved and critical. "If Briand," he said, "wants to impose a formula for European union from without, instead of drawing it from the reality of the situation, he will fail . . . In my opinion, he has put the question badly. He ought to have started on solid ground, where the European federation has already begun to form, on the economic ground. From the economic cooperation, already very close, of a few European states, European unity would come, developing constantly, and the other states would have rallied to it one after the other."

The events which followed a brief period of entente no longer concern the figures of Stresemann and Briand, who soon disappeared. Whatever their respective merit may have been, their goals, their vision of a future which required a Franco–German accord, could they have done more than they did? In a period of time as short as that in which they were active, Stresemann could do no more than ask for concessions, which his fellow-citizens found insufficient. It was difficult for Briand to grant more or to do it more quickly; even if he had been willing, he did not have the means, since France was not behind him. The two peoples had opposing conceptions of a treaty which one considered just and applicable, while the other found it intolerable, dishonoring, and impossible to execute. And so destiny followed its course, willing that German pride should be more satisfied with the destruction of the Treaty of Versailles than by arrangements freely discussed with the partner, and that the French would be less shocked at allowing what they thought was theirs to be taken from them than they would have been in giving it freely. They put up with Hitler more easily than with Stresemann, preferring to undergo the violence of a madman rather than demonstrate generosity and daring.

[57]Particularly, the popular election of the president of the republic (Marshal Hindenburg was elected), and also Article 48, which granted the president full powers in certain circumstances.

[58]We really mean the German nationalists, not the German people. Many Germans were aware of their defeat, and first among them were William II, who fled to Holland, and the military leaders, who asked for the armistice. Simple common sense indicated that a Hindenburg or a Ludendorff would not have capitulated if they had not thought they were defeated. The nationalists, on the other hand, thought up the legend of the "stab in the back" which eventually won many adherents.

[59]The idea, rather widespread outside of Germany, that Hitler may have been only the instrument of heavy industry and the militarists is not at all realistic. The truth is that he used both groups as soon as he became strong enough to convince them that it was to their interest to rally to his cause. He obtained his financing from the manufacturers, then used the army to carry out his plans for conquest. Both the big industrialists and the militarists obeyed him, although neither group belonged to the small clique which surrounded him, exercising absolute power with him.

[60]Stresemann wrote in his *Notebooks:* "The first draft of the preliminary agreement contained the expression

'maintenance of the status quo.' We influenced the Allies to substitute the word 'peace' for this . . . We said that we were not seeking to obtain a change in the existing treaties. We did add, however, that those treaties could not constitute an untouchable legal statute. In other words, we were saying that we were not expressing any moral renunciation."

[61]Stresemann had said: "The Polish Corridor is like a wall separating the lover and his beloved," and when asked if Poland could give it up, he answered: "There are men in Poland just as there are anywhere else."

He did not dare raise the question with Pilsudsky, however, whom he met at Geneva in 1927. When Chamberlain asked him to do it, he replied, "I cannot ask a man I don't know point blank for a piece of his bread."

[62]The German word *finassiren* does not correspond exactly to the French *finasser* (to resort to trickery); infrequent (it does not appear in most dictionaries), it has a less pejorative shade of meaning. Used particularly in reference to fencing, it means to execute a feint.

CHAPTER 12

Hitler and France

WE shall not dwell on Hitler's rise to power, nor on his domestic or foreign policy, which are all rather well known.[63] It appears of greater interest to examine his attitude toward France and that of France toward him.

Everyone knows that France and England, making no more than vain protests, allowed Hitler to decree obligatory military service in 1935, in violation of the Treaty of Versailles. In 1936, they let him occupy the demilitarized zone of the Rhineland, in violation of the treaty and of the Locarno Pact. In 1938, they allowed him to annex Austria, again in violation of treaties, and agreed some months later to his taking the Sudetens from Czechoslovakia. There resulted from these successive capitulations a serious responsibility for France and England in the events which would follow in

World War II. When one sees danger coming and stands with his arms folded, he mustn't be surprised when the catastrophe happens.

Is it too early to talk of individual responsibilities? We are tempted to think so, since no one else talks of them. There were leaders of government in England as well as in France; if, up to the present, neither people has wanted to ask its leaders for an accounting, that is their affair. Let us leave to posterity the responsibility of finding the details, since all the documents have not yet been published.

What were Hitler's views on France? He was such a blunt, simple man that they are rather easily defined.

His *idée fixe* was German expansion to the east. All of his foreign policy, as he revealed it in *Mein Kampf*, as he put it into practice in attacking Poland, then the U.S.S.R., was subordinated to this principal idea. He thought that the German people needed more than anything else "living space," room which in his view could be found only in that direction. It was in this spirit that he criticized all the history of Germany, reproaching various princes and emperors for having sought to expand to the south and the west, thus wasting strength they might have used for the *Drang nach Osten* (Drive to the East).

From this point of view, France could have only a secondary interest for him. He treated her very badly in *Mein Kampf*, written during the occupation of the Ruhr when Gallophobia was raging throughout Germany. France's military action and the fact that she controlled the armed might of Europe gave reason to believe that she would oppose any

German expansion, and that consequently she would have
to be put out of action before anything at all could be
attempted. On the other hand, he remained faithful to the
old German thesis of a France trying to get the Rhineland
boundary, despite the fact that the Treaty of Versailles had
been limited to the demilitarization of the left bank of the
Rhine. Hitler wrote in 1924:

> The mortal enemy, the implacable enemy of the
> German people, is and continues to be France. What-
> ever her regime, Bourbons or Jacobins, little Napoleons,
> Republicans, ecclesiastics or red Bolshevists, the aim
> of her foreign policy will always be to seize the Rhine
> border, to insure its possession of this river by dividing
> and crushing Germany. England would like to see to it
> that Germany should not be a world power, France that
> she should not even be a power. That is a capital dif-
> ference . . .
>
> The alliance with England and Italy would give
> Germany the possibility of proceeding quietly with those
> preparations which, in the structure of such a coalition,
> will have to be made in any case for a settlement of ac-
> counts with France . . . *on condition, however, that Ger-
> many sees in the annihilation of France only a means of
> procuring for our people the possibility of expanding
> elsewhere . . .*

Those lines are clear enough. France must be eliminated because she is an intruder, but she is not a goal for conquest.
Some years later, in 1930, Hitler would express himself differently. He had been able to observe that France was thinking
neither of splitting up Germany nor of conquering the left
bank of the Rhine; as a matter of fact, she had just withdrawn

her troops. On the other hand, already foreseeing his coming to power, Hitler wanted to give reassurances. On October 24, 1930, he set forth in his official newspaper, the *Völkische Beobachter,* his conception of Franco–German relations. All Germans, he said, were hoping for improvement and wanted to live at peace with all civilized nations.

Are we to say that this was merely the language of hypocrisy? It goes without saying that if Hitler took over the government of an almost unarmed country, he would have to deal tactfully with his neighbors, and France first of all; but he also had to gauge German policy to French policy, and if France appeared less threatening than she had six years earlier, it is logical to suppose that he might have changed his plans concerning her.

At that time he could ask himself if his projects for expansion to the east might not be feasible with France's neutrality, which would spare Germany a costly operation in the west. This feeling could only have been strengthened when he saw, after he had become master of Germany, that France was not reacting to a single one of his undertakings. If she allowed him to rearm, to annex Austria, to destroy Czechoslovakia, apparently she had no desire to intervene against him. The French were less interested in communist Russia than in their allies in Central Europe; if they abandoned them, why should they mobilize in favor of Moscow, or even in favor of Poland? If Poland was her ally, so was Czechoslovakia, and hadn't she abandoned her?

During this period, Hitler made an effort to placate France. "He is effusive," wrote M. François–Poncet, "in kind words for her, in assurance of esteem and of a desire for reconciliation. He even goes so far as to declare that his finest title to glory would be that someday a monument might be built honoring him as the conciliator of the two countries."[64] In conversation with Frenchmen, he asserted that Germany had definitely given up Alsace–Lorraine; to an Englishman, that he was ready to sign a defensive alliance with England, in order to give security to France.[65] He advocated direct contacts between German and French people and established a France–Germany Society. With Poland, France's ally, he signed a non-aggression and consultation pact (January 26, 1934). In *Mein Kampf*, Poland was not even mentioned— a disturbing silence, in view of the fact that expansion eastward could not be carried out without marching over her.[66] There had been no common border between Germany and Russia since 1919.

In 1938 and 1939, events, which were successful for Hitler, had moved so swiftly that it was difficult to know how his plans and projects were being modified. It is well known that following Munich, he asked Poland to cede Danzig, along with permission to build a highway through the corridor; then he asked for the entire corridor.[67]

To understand the attitude of France we must go back a little further. The Franco–Polish alliance dated from 1921. An attempt to revise it had been made in 1927 at the instigation of the general staff. The Polish government refused all discussion, arguing that the accord was immutable, and the French government yielded. A new opportunity for revising the alliance arose in 1936, when Hitler occupied the demilitarized zone of the Rhineland and denounced the Locarno Pact. France had thus lost the pawn which allowed her to begin a war with Germany under favorable conditions. Since her purely defensive strategy was based on the Maginot Line, her aid to Poland became problematical if the latter were attacked. Would holding down a few German divisions on our border be enough to assist Poland effectively? Was it normal that of two allies, the weaker should be forced to the greater effort, while the more powerful one, entrenched behind a fortified line, should watch the other do the fighting? This plan was both absurd and humiliating to those who had conceived it. Perhaps the Poles would not have accepted it if they had not thought that the French army would quickly take the offensive and would use its fortifications only as a base. This was, of course, an erroneous assumption.[68]

The alliance was seriously questioned in 1938, after Munich. Since Poland had occupied the Czech district of Teschen, which belonged to Czechoslovakia, an ally of France, could this not have been taken as a pretext for denouncing the Polish alliance? France does not appear to have reacted energetically at the time. Although a move was considered for a while, and although Ambassador Noël favored a certain limitation of the alliance, which would have been replaced with a pact of friendship and consultation and with a military accord of limited scope, this rectification was not accepted in Paris. The policy of "hands free in the east" was considered dangerous; it was thought that it would throw Poland into the arms of Germany and would not protect France from conflict. In truth, such a policy would have forced Poland to make concessions, and wasn't that preferable to world war? Poland was prevented from reaching an understanding with Germany. The result was to bring Russia and Germany together against Poland, and the ultimate result, a hundred times worse, was the Hitler–Stalin accord of August 23, 1939, a veritable treaty for the division of Poland between Germany and the U.S.S.R. At the same time, it demolished all of France's strategic plans.

France had counted on Soviet Russia to fill out the eighty Polish divisions which were to fight in the east against Germany. The Franco–Soviet pact of May 2, 1935, required France and the U.S.S.R. to assist each other in case of German aggression. This pact was pure illusion; it carried no military accord, it did not require the U.S.S.R. to intervene if Germany attacked Poland, which was the most likely *casus belli,* and finally, Russia, having no common border with Germany, could do nothing against her except through Poland, and therefore could act only with Poland's consent. One of two possibilities could occur—either Germany would attack Poland, and in that case, Moscow could say, "The matter does not concern me, my alliance is with France," or Germany could attack France, and Poland could say, "I do not permit the Russian army to cross my territory."

Naturally Paris and London had seen the danger. Since the situation had deteriorated since Munich, the Western powers tried to insure the U.S.S.R.'s support, which implied a refocusing of the Franco–Soviet treaty. A diplomatic and military negotiation began in Moscow, at the very moment that the Soviets were carrying on negotiations with Germany.

France and Germany

Franco–British diplomacy has been criticized for having been unaware of this double game, for having allowed itself to be duped by its partner. Is this criticism justified? Dispatches from Coulondre, the ambassador from France to Berlin, announced Soviet–German conversations as early as the month of May, and at the same time there was open talk of them in the press, at least in Berlin newspaper circles. It is even asserted that as early as January, the United States ambassador, Mr. Bullitt, informed the French government of them. But what more could be done than to go on with the negotiation and to try to overcome the enormous difficulties? The diplomatic accord was concluded on July 25; by obtaining a Soviet guaranty not only for Poland but also for several small countries, it was by and large satisfactory. But the military accord failed, Poland absolutely refusing to authorize the crossing of its territory by Soviet troops. From that point on, Germany had won. On August 21, Ribbentrop's departure for Moscow was learned, and two days later the nonaggression pact between Germany and the U.S.S.R. was signed. It meant that the U.S.S.R. withdrew in advance from the threatening conflict leaving France, England, and Poland to face Germany alone.

A controversy still goes on over whether or not the Soviets ever really intended to deal with England and France. Beck has always asserted that they were determined to do nothing, and that they took the Polish refusal as a pretext, their negotiations with the western powers being only a feint to hide their conversations with Germany. This is possible, but one might answer the Polish minister that he would have backed the Soviets against the wall if he had accepted passage of their troops through Poland. By stubbornly refusing to do this, he had made all military aid impossible, and had rendered the Franco–Polish alliance inapplicable. What was the use of letting France and England negotiate in Moscow, if the negotiation was leading into an impasse?[69]

Two weeks before the war, Minister Bonnet asked Mr. Lukasiewicz if his country had any fortified positions facing Germany; the Polish ambassador replied that this was not necessary: "The Polish army will invade Germany in the first days of war." There was less optimism in Paris. With the situation reversed by the defection of the U.S.S.R.,[70] some wondered finally if the Franco–Polish alliance might not be reconsidered. It was for this purpose that a war council was convoked as soon as the conclusion of the German–Soviet pact was known. The question was whether France was capable of making war with only Poland's support. The British army was not ready and could not be taken into account for several months. Finding the answer was more the responsibility of the military men than of the politicians. The following is based on the minutes of this meeting, written by General Decamps:

To the question, "Are the army, the navy, and the air force capable of honoring our engagements?" General Gamelin and Admiral Darlan answered "yes," without reservations; M. Guy La Chambre declared less categorically that our air force had made great progress. (In reality, we were building two hundred planes a month, but everything is relative—the Germans were building a thousand.)

To the question, "Is it better to be faithful to our engagements and go to war now, or to reconsider our attitude and profit from the delay thus obtained to increase our military strength, since it is clearly understood that France runs the risk of being attacked in its turn within a period of only a few months?" Gamelin answered that he believed "in an honorable resistance by Poland and by Roumania,[71] which would prevent the mass of the German forces from turning back against us before next spring. France therefore has no choice. The solution to be faced is that of holding to our commitments to Poland." The general in chief added that at the beginning of hostilities the ground forces and the navy could do little against Germany. "On the other hand, French mobilization will of itself bring some relief to Poland, by holding on our borders a certain number of German units."

It would seem difficult to be more heavily mistaken than the general in chief of the French army. In short, he was of the opinion that war should be undertaken immediately, because France had nothing to fear from Germany before spring. Poland would take it upon herself to hold Germany in check. Poland, however, would be crushed in nineteen days. France ought to have helped her by pinning down large German units, but she held down only a small number of divisions; the Germans, knowing that we would not attack, left only a thin curtain of troops on the French front. Gamelin had asserted that our army was capable of honoring our commitments, but, under his command at least, it showed itself to be no more capable than the Polish army. Moreover, when it really had to face Germany, our commitments had expired, since the Polish state had ceased to exist.

Are we to say that the military advisers were right in saying that France risked coming under attack in her turn within a few months? She would indeed be attacked, but France and England had declared the war themselves—what could the enemy do but fight them?

An interesting question, which the general and the French government might have asked themselves, and which they do not seem to have asked, is this: "Would Hitler have gone to war in the west after having won in the east, if France and England had not forced him to it by opening hostilities against him?" Up to now, we do not know the answer, and perhaps we shall never know.[72]

It is possible that Hitler considerd this war inevitable, in order to protect his rear during his major operation which would be the campaign against Russia. It might also be that he would have preferred to hold all his forces in reserve for that campaign. We must not forget, first, that the Franco–British alliance required him to face both France and England, and that he had always wanted to placate the latter. The German fleet was made up basically of thirteen large fighting ships, against one hundred seven British and French ships; secondly, that neither Hitler nor his general staff counted on the swift victory of 1940. Let us not judge his intentions according to a success which no one had foreseen. The Germans thought that the French army would hold behind the Maginot Line, that the war might be a long and costly one. Why would they have exhausted their forces against the western powers, instead of saving them for the only enterprise which had always been Hitler's heart—expansion to the east?

Before September 1, 1939, he had achieved many victories, and without ever fighting. The Polish campaign, in his view, was to be a limited operation, intended to complete the enlargement of the Reich. A conflict with England and France was of quite a different character. It was a fight against two great powers, which might become, as the 1914 experience had shown, a European and world war. Germany would have to engage in it with all her strength, losing sight of the precise goal of conquering lands inside Russia, which Hitler had set for himself. The result was doubtful, for the German army of 1939 was not what we imagine; it was nothing like the Kaiser's. It was a force which had been improvised in four years, with young, well-trained conscript classes, good morale, good equipment, but it had no reserves. Victory over Franco–British coalition was not at all certain for Hitler, and it does not seem logical to think that he necessarily had to attack it, since his essential goals lay elsewhere.[73]

Such aggression was contrary to his interest, and those who claim that he had to act without considering his interest reveal their superficiality. Up to that time, Hitler had shown that his acts were carefully calculated. This time, it is true, he erred in his calculations, if he was counting on the abstention of England and France. Didn't they commit another error, if they thought he would inevitably have declared war, and if they might have avoided it?

Their principal argument is that they were committed to aiding Poland, England by Chamberlain's statement of March 31, France by its treaty alliance. Coulondre, the French ambassador to Berlin, wrote in his *Mémoires:* "The Franco–Polish alliance was to become automatically operative in case of aggression against either power. This automatic character having been formally and repeatedly brought to the notice of the German government, the Reich had placed itself in a state of war with France, and not France with the Reich." Such diplomatic and juridicial subtleties do not prevent a treaty of alliance, if it was made to be honored, from being honored honestly if the ally whose aid is required is really capable of giving it.[74] In 1938 and in 1939, France had made no gesture to defend the independence of her ally Czechoslovakia, a question of capital importance. Was it necessary that she fight for the Danzig Corridor, a geographic monster doomed from the moment it was spawned? Events have provided the answer—France was not capable of coming to Poland's aid. One may say that it is easy to judge this after the fact, but it was clear from the beginning that it would be so. You don't win a war by putting your hands in your pockets while a weaker ally takes all the enemy's blows. To the lightning offensive by Germany against Poland the only effective reply was an immediate attack in kind along the Franco–German front. It was all the more appropriate because the Germans, having taken the majority of their forces to the east, had only forty divisions at the most against eighty French divisions.[75] These French divisions buried themselves in the Maginot Line, and the French army witnessed as a spectator Poland's death throes which lasted a scant three weeks. It has been claimed that the Siegfried Line was impregnable, whereas it was in reality only a paper curtain, a simple bluff, as the Germans themselves have said.[76] Were the Germans stopped by the Maginot Line? Just as they went around it later, so could the French armies then have gone through Belgium and Holland without violating their neutrality, for Articles 16 and 17 of the League of Nations Pact required its members to allow the passage of troops marching against an aggressor.[77]

A French counterattack was possible, despite certain inferiorities in armaments, which were less serious, moreover, than they have been said to be. It was necessary that the French army, like the German army, be placed swiftly on a war footing, but mobilization would continue up to September 15, whereas the Germans, after forty-eight hours, already occupied a part of Poland.

And that is the true cause of the defeat—a strategic plan which provided for a purely defensive action, or in other words, a delaying action with a minimum effort. Perhaps it could have been enough if Germany had been faced, in the east, by an opponent like Russia, with her larger population and huge expanse of territory; but in the case of Poland, if the French thought to be an ally by staying home, they misunderstood the sense of their alliance. The only possible action was an energetic and swift offensive. Rather than apply the alliance as they did, wouldn't it have been better to denounce it at the appropriate time, and to work on the ally to prevent the *casus foederis* from happening? Poland was obliged to

126

come to an understanding with Germany; she would no doubt have lost the corridor thereby, but this was still better than losing her freedom.

What are we to think of the peace offer which Hitler, according to certain statements, is said to have made after his victory over Poland? It was first formulated in respect to England in the speech given by Hitler to the Reichstag on October 6, 1939. "Hitler," M. François–Poncet writes, "proceeded to several soundings of opinion with France and England in order to stop at the point which had been reached. He was told that they would never deal with him."[78] More explicitly, Ambassador Bullitt related in one of his reports that "Goering has asked an American industrialist, Mr. James Mooney, director of the foreign services of General Motors, to transmit to Paris and London the suggestion for a meeting on neutral ground of representatives of the German, British, and French governments with a view toward studying the possibilities for peace."[79] Was the proposal really transmitted, and by whom and in what terms? Precisely what answer was made to it? Were there any contacts between Paris and London on this matter? None of these points, so far as is known, has ever been answered; the silence of the persons who do know is astonishing. It would be interesting to know what Hitler's true intentions were. Did he envisage proposals which could really be discussed, or was it a maneuver, intended to slow down the French and English military preparations while he pushed his own forward? According to the diaries of General Jodl, chief of operations, and of General Halder, chief of staff of the ground forces, heated discussions may have occurred in October and November, 1939, on the matter of an offensive plan in the west. This offensive, planned for the autumn, may have been deferred several times, and did not take place until May, 1940.

Military preparations are not incompatible with diplomatic activity. As long as diplomatic activity has not begun, or as long as it has produced no results once begun, preparations cannot be interrupted. The command, as long as war is in progress, can do no more than take measures for getting on with it.

Nothing proves that at that time Hitler was not disposed to deal. One would have liked to know on what conditions, even if they were unacceptable. His goal, which was to strike Poland, was attained; in nineteen days he had made himself its master, more easily, more rapidly than he had dared hope. France and England had scarcely reacted. At the very most it can be said that during this period there were some hostilities between them and Germany, so that the psychological conditions which would permit cessation of hostilities were not lacking. But by the very fact that they themselves had declared war—even though they were not really waging it— it was difficult for them to end it. Had they continued to wait, if for only two weeks, after Germany's entry into war, they could perhaps have abstained, could have consolidated and reserved their forces, could have been in a better position if Hitler attacked them later. It is not very likely that he would have done so, with Poland annihilated. They then could have acted in complete freedom on the day when he would march

against Russia, and could have entered the fray in their turn
if they deemed it necessary.

Although the behavior of the French and British governments seem indefensible from the point of view of political
reason, it could be explained psychologically. After having
put up with Hitler's insults, his treaty violations, his acts of
force, they behaved like the weak individual who changes
abruptly from a pattern of extreme cowardice to one of extreme violence, finally doing something desperate after having
taken the blows and the insults. Their only excuse, if it is one
at all, is that on September 1, 1939, a decision which was both
honorable and reasonable no longer appeared possible. Things
had been allowed to go so far that it was thought that the
only choice was to give up or to accept the catastrophe; the
choice was catastrophe, and it was the end of a long chain
which people had been busily forging for years.

The first link of this chain was Versailles, when the ab-
surb notion of the Danzig Corridor leapt full blown from the
statesmen's heads. It was continued with a policy of allying
oneself with Poland, supporting her against the Germans instead of exhorting her to come to an agreement with them.
In Pilsudski and Beck, Poland had leaders who were rather
well disposed toward their western neighbor. They could
have found a *modus vivendi*, and before Hitler's time. But
the Poles thought they should root their intransigence in an
alliance which would prove fatal to them.

When their policy of resistance had been pushed to the
limit, an attempt was made to shore it up against a Russia of
which neither the real strength nor the real intentions were

known. Over Chamberlain and Daladier she preferred Hitler; rather than help Poland against him, she preferred to return to the old policy of the czars, the policy of partition.

That everything about this new Franco–German conflict had been falsified from the very beginning was something the French people felt utterly. That is why they talked about the "phony war" and showed such little enthusiasm for getting on with it. We might say that this war did develop differently than had been foreseen, and that, in addition, it ended in the victory of Hitler's opponents, and that this cancels out all the rest—the initial collapse, the occupation, the deportations, the deaths and the destruction, the crash of the French and British empires and of certain others. It remains to be discovered if the French people might not have preferred to see Nazis in Berlin, even in Danzig, rather than undergo four years of their more immediate presence; it remains to be learned if the Polish people would not willingly have given up the corridor, rather than become the slaves of the communists.

Victories due fundamentally to others, as well as to unforeseeable combinations of circumstances do not efface errors. It would be serious for the future of a people, if it thought that having taken a decision based not on reason and calculation, but rather on shame and despair, it was performing an act of consummate political wisdom. If Hitler's policy toward France, and even more so his policy toward Czechoslovakia and Poland, was execrable, France's policy, from the day she did not make war on him when she could, to the day she did make war when she couldn't, was always completely absurd.

[63]It might be more accurate to say "rather *badly* known." What people do know is the story of the major events marking twelve years of national socialism. Concerning the fundamental nature of this regime we often develop false, or at least incomplete, ideas. Authoritarianism, anti-semitism, and nationalism are not enough to define it, and we err in contrasting it as a regime of the extreme right to the communist extreme left. A certain social policy had an important place in Hitler's program, which was after all called "national-socialist." Although circumstances at first forced him to subordinate socialism to nationalism, the time for socialism would come later. If Hitler had lived, he might have evolved toward a kind of national-communism. He had no ties to the so-called capitalist class, and although at one time he tried to humor it, this was merely a matter of tactics to get the support he needed. When his regime was firmly established on the two main pillars of the party and the police, he was no longer dependent on any class. He was free to rely on the one he thought would give him the best support. There is little doubt that with modern developments in a big industrial country like Germany, he would have preferred the working class to the middle class. Other dictators, Peron, for example, relied on the working class.

[64]From *De Versailles à Potsdam.*

[65]Wouldn't such an alliance have been made superfluous by the Locarno Pact, to which England was signatory and which Hitler would denounce in 1936? Are we to believe that when he made the statements cited, he did not know what it contained? It's quite a likely possibility.

[66]As a matter of fact, Poland is mentioned twice, but very briefly, in allusions to its Germanization in the past, and not in reference to Hitler's plans.

[67]This negotiation can be followed in the correspondence of Lipski, the Polish ambassador to Berlin, with his minister, Beck (*Relations polono-allemandes, 1933-1939*), and in that of the German ambassador to Warsaw, Moltke, with the secretary of state, Mackensen. The German demands kept growing steadily. The negotiation was still being conducted after March 31, 1939, when England gave a public guaranty to Poland and Hitler replied to it by denouncing the Polish–German Pact of 1934.

[68]On the very day war was declared, Lukasiewicz, the Polish ambassador to Paris, would make urgent representations to the French government to have the French army attack along the whole western front.

[69]It seems, however, that Poland envisaged the possibility of help from the Soviet air force and of being supplied with weapons and munitions, which would prove that she was not counting on a total abstention on the part of the U.S.S.R. and still less on a veritable Germano–Soviet alliance aimed at her destruction as an independent state.

[70]"The diplomatic and military situation has been upset from top to bottom," wrote George Bonnet. "The Polish government has played its game without concerning itself about its partners."

[71]Roumania was not attacked by Germany.

[72]No document published so far allows us to form any definite opinion.

[73]Certain statements appear to confirm this hypothesis of a possible abstention:

Bonnet to German Ambassador Welczek, July 1, 1938: "England and France are bound by public commitments and will immediately be at Poland's side if she is attacked."

Welczek to Bonnet: "I am repeating it to my government. I am having some difficulty in convincing it. It cannot understand how England and France would commit this folly . . . We have faced the risk of a European war and have built up considerable reserves."

Ribbentrop to Bonnet, July 13, 1939: "The Führer has always desired Franco–German entente, but if the French government wants war, it will find Germany at every moment."

Hitler to Coulondre, August 25, 1939: "I will not attack France, but if she enters the conflict, I will go all the way."

[74]See above (p. 125) our discussion of the conditional nature of alliances.

[75]Other estimates have been published, for example, those of Marshal Keitel and General Jodl, who evaluated the French divisions at one hundred ten, the German at only twenty-five, including those in reserve.

[76]The German writer Walter Goerlitz, as quoted by Colonel Goutard in *1940, la guerre des occasions manquées,* wrote: "General Gamelin could not believe that these fortifications were fundamentally a huge bluff." A great deal of evidence confirms this opinion.

[77]Without using the many technical works which describe the German offensive of 1940 and the French defeat, the reader may consult, in addition to the excellent work cited above, those of Benoist-Méchin, *60 jours qui ébranlèrent l' Occident* and *La Bataille de France.*

It will be seen that our authors have been more interested in the battle of May and June, 1940; if it had been won, it would not have prevented Poland's defeat, which dated from 1939, and would not have furnished any means of rectifying that situation, since that country had been divided up between Russia and Germany. France and England could not go to war against Russia and Germany at the same time. Consequently, the objective of the war, which was to save Poland, could not in any case have been achieved. It was in September, 1939, not in May, 1940, that France should have fought.

[78]From *De Versailles à Potsdam.*

[79]*Le Monde,* February 28, 1956.

CHAPTER 13

Conqueror Without Conquests

HITLER's conquests were of two kinds—those resulting from Pan-Germanism, consisting of the annexations of territories inhabited by Germans (Austria, the Sudetenland, Memel) and those aimed at enlarging German "living space," made essentially at the expense of the Slavs, driving them eastward.

The first was quickly achieved without opposition. Had Hitler stopped there, he could have lived quietly in a Germany enlarged without war by nearly sixty-two thousand square miles and by ten million inhabitants; this was indeed a huge success.[80] Outside Germany, Pan-Germanism had always been considered an intolerable and subversive doctrine, but the powers accepted its application without reacting.

134

Hitler, it is true, had not carried Pan-Germanism to its absolute logical conclusion; he could not claim the South Tyrol, annexed by Italy in 1918, without falling out with his friend Mussolini; he could not claim Alsace without going to war with France; he could not claim Switzerland, Luxembourg, or the Netherlands without provoking England and all Europe. And so, dropping the Pan-Germanist program, he found it less dangerous to seize Czechoslovakia, next Poland, and finally when those ventures had succeeded, to attack Russia; the big operation designed to take "living space" from the Slavs had begun.

Would he have reached his goal if he had avoided war in the west, first with England and France then with the United States? It is possible but not certain. After the initial advance made by the German army, Soviet forces showed that they were superior to what he had expected; if we take into account the vastness which Russia has always turned against conquerors, the struggle might have ended in a stalemate in which the two opponents would have exhausted each other.

It ended in a defeat unprecedented in German history. After twenty-three years of war and the defeat at Waterloo, France had returned to her former boundaries, but now, Germany lost a fourth of her territory, which was annexed to Poland and the U.S.S.R. (without counting Austria and the Sudetenland, acquired by Germany in 1938 and now taken from her). What she had left was cut in two, and no one could tell when the eastern and western parts might be reunited. More than twelve million Germans, living beyond the Oder-Neisse Line and in Czechoslovakia, were pushed back into this mutilated Germany.

A few statistics will give a more exact idea of the German disaster:

Germany in 1914 .... 540,000 sq. kms.
Germany in 1919 (after Versailles) .. 468,000 sq. kms.
Germany in 1945 .... 355,000 sq. kms.

Of the 1945 figure, 248 thousand sq. kms. are in the Federal Republic, and 107 thousand in the People's (Democratic) Republic.

German territory, practically equal under William II to that of France, was thus reduced to three-fifths of its former size. German losses of territory corresponded to the area of thirty French departments. The Federal Republic is barely half the size of France. German population has varied little since 1914; the losses of the two wars were offset by an excess of births and by the influx of refugees from the east. It is still around seventy million, but its density has increased in East Germany from 130 to 203 inhabitants per square kilometer. A comparison of these figures with those for Slavic countries has a certain interest: Slavic countries other than the U.S.S.R.: 850 thousand sq. kms., with a population of 60 million (70 to the sq. km.); the U.S.S.R.: 22 million sq. kms., with a population of 206 million (9 to the sq. km.).[81]

It should be noted that at the end of the last war, the U.S.S.R. gained 684 thousand sq. kms.; these areas were taken from nine different countries: Finland, Esthonia, Latvia, Lithuania, Poland, Germany, Czechoslovakia, Roumania, and Japan.

These figures show that (1) while Germany lost twenty-five per cent of its territory in the Second World War, the

U.S.S.R., already the largest country in the world, increased its territory by an area twice the size of Germany; the Soviet Union is seventy times as large as all Germany, one hundred times larger than West Germany; (2) Germany has a population density over twenty times greater than Russia's; (3) the Slavic countries other than Russia, with an area almost twice that of Germany, have a total population which is lower than Germany's.

The figures Hitler had before him were not quite the same; they were less unfavorable to Germany. Nevertheless, he found them enough to justify his plans for conquest. His attempt failed. In trying to be the great conqueror, the greatest in all German history, he succeeded in reducing Germany to the smallest dimensions she has over had. A conclusion less cruel for him, since he is no longer here to comtemplate his handiwork, than it is for the people he threw into this adventure. Yet we might wonder, on going back over the centuries, if the epithet "conqueror without conquests" might not apply to the whole German people.

We have already noted[82] that the big Germanic invasions were by and large failures. The Germans had missed a great opportunity, that of inheriting the Roman Empire. When it collapsed, they represented the only warlike power in the world of that time; they had the support of the Church, the only spiritual force, the guardian of western civilization, and the principal link among the inhabitants of the fallen empire. These elements would have permitted the creation of a great new power which the Germans could not create by themselves. They did not yet have, as the Romans had had, the idea of the state, since they were nothing but a collection of tribes. One of them, the Franks, was able to found a great kingdom, an empire in fact, but it did not endure. Its leaders destroyed it themselves. When a German king made a second attempt, he established the Holy Roman Germanic Empire which knew its moment of glory, declined, then revived with the Hapsburgs, but never finally became either a great German national state nor a multi-national state; it varied between the two. That was no doubt one of the major causes of its failure.

It was already too late in our times to create a German empire. One had existed in the Middle Ages and had broken up; the Holy Roman Empire had originally included Switzerland, Alsace, Luxembourg, the Netherlands, Austria— all Germanic countries—and in addition, certain non-Germanic countries such as Lorraine, Wallonia, and Bohemia. It was unable even to retain its German components and it continued to crumble away all along its periphery. Certain provinces, such as Alsace, were taken from it by a neighboring kingdom, but others, such as Switzerland, Holland, and Belgium, separated from it by themselves. The last straw was when Bismarck, about to found a new German empire, excluded Austria from it; only a few years before, at the Frankfort Parliament, Austria had sought to be united to Germany. Today the Germanic countries separated from Germany include thirty-five million inhabitants, half the population of Germany itself.

Although some countries still have national islands outside their borders, none has such important ones as Germany.

This fact is apparently explained by the absence, over the centuries, of a unified and strong German state. It is her prolonged divisions, the scattering into multiple sovereignties, and the impotency of her emperors which have prevented her from watching over the integrity of her territory. While French royal power was constantly enlarging its territory, Germany's domain continued to decrease. This progressive shrinking of German territory explains to a certain extent the claims of the Pan-Germanists, who desired the return of lost provinces to Germany; unfortunately, their theory gave no heed to history. There are historic hours for forming a nation, but if they are allowed to pass by, they become so many lost opportunities. It would have been relatively easy for Germany to keep the territories which are now detached from her. Could anyone imagine today the possibility of bringing Switzerland or the Netherlands back into the German circle? A spirit and traditions have developed in these peoples, very different from the German spirit and traditions, and Holland has even developed another language.

Historians have thought they could see a spontaneous grouping of populations of the same nationality around a national hub. This phenomenon indubitably does occur. But there is also, in some cases, an inverse movement, which seems equally spontaneous. We are surprised to see with what ease a territory detached from the national body by the hazard of events becomes accustomed to living in separation. In 1918, Austria would have decided by an overwhelming majority for *Anschluss* with Germany; today, she no longer gives it a thought[83] French-speaking Switzerland, Walloon Belgium, the Anglo–Norman islands where French is spoken, think just as little about joining France. After 1870, could Alsace not have been formed into a new Switzerland, had France and Germany so desired?

The expansionist policy of Prussia and the Hapsburgs generally attracts more attention than these successive relinquishments of German lands. The Hapsburgs annexed the kingdoms of Bohemia, Hungary, and diverse Slavic territories; they long occupied Northern Italy; the margraves of Brandenburg and the Knights of the Teutonic Order expanded to the east and the northeast, destroying or assimilating the Slav populations. The Austrians and the Prussians would one day divide Poland with the czar. The Hapsburg policy of marriages and inheritances carried them also into the west, toward Burgundy and Spain, but this growth at the expense of foreign peoples ended only in a false facade and a false power. All the foreign conquests of Prussia, like those of Austria, were destined to disappear, while losses of German lands would never be recovered, and the balance sheets of Germany's territorial policy would be entirely negative. A great people, big enough, warlike enough to defend its space against its neighbors, and even to enlarge it, would finally see itself concentrated, crowded inside narrow borders, stripped not only of what did not properly belong to it, but also of territories which it had populated and exploited for centuries.

Are we to think that from the Germanic invasions to Hitler, these two opposite movements have never ceased, that we are still observing today the same lack of measure, the same tendency to excessive aggrandizements which by that very fact are unattainable, and at the same time, the giving up of German lands which normally ought not to have taken place? These two movements could be linked to the same cause, to the division of Germany into several sovereign states which gave her several policies, rather than a single, unified policy. These states constantly changed their boundaries, inwardly and outwardly; those on the outer edges sometimes found it easier to expand outside of Germany. This was particularly the case of Prussia and of Austria. There was no geographic conception of the German nation, of a territory corresponding to the habitat of the German people, and which all Germans would have worked to defend. It was not very important that Germany had few or almost no natural boundaries. Poland, Belgium, Holland, and other countries do not have them either. If Germany was not bounded in any exact way by a given river or range of mountains, she was bounded *grosso modo* by the area which Germans occupied. Had they clung to that with all their strength and without encroaching upon their neighbors, they could have kept the German lands as their land.

Is it a matter of chance that the greatest withdrawal of Germany occurred after its strongest forward push? No one knows—Hitler himself perhaps did not know—how far he would have taken his conquests if he had been able to go on. The Russian space was immense, and conquests could have gone far. He announced his intention to evacuate the conquered territories in order to populate them with Germans, and he probably would have done it. His mass murders of millions of Jews, Poles, even Germans, show that nothing would have stopped him. The whole unsuccessful operation backfired against him, or rather after his death, against the German people.

We have witnessed the return of the eastern boundary of Germany to the Oder, which it had passed in the fourteenth century, and the driving of ten million Germans from provinces they had occupied for five hundred years. Among the exiles were three million Sudeten Germans who had been settled in northern Bohemia from the earliest times. In no one's memory had such huge populations been displaced following a war. Although the Germans had formulated this kind of project, it was their opponents who carried it out.

Are we to see in all of this a just reversal of the order of things? Justice, however, has nothing to do with this situation; so long as a proposed injustice has not been consummated, one cannot use it as a basis for justifying revenge. Let us say rather than the Russians and the Poles took Hitler's plans as a pretext for helping themselves at Germany's expense. The Russians had not hesitated in 1939 to divide Poland with Germany; they now kept what they had taken and reimbursed Poland with the eastern German provinces and their inhabitants. Perhaps in doing this they have set a dangerous precedent. In former times which we call barbarous, a territory was annexed and those who lived there were left there; today they are driven out, a more radical and simpler solution. However, there is no longer any guaranty that after another war the Germans will not drive out in their turn the ten million Poles, Czechs, and Russians, or even drive out the French, if they judge it more convenient to expand to the west rather than to the east.

It is true that the new solution has its advantages. If Louis XIV, after taking Alsace, had replaced the Alsatians with Bretons and people from Marseille, the Germans would no doubt have ceased to claim it. In the same manner, if Bismarck had driven out the Gallicized Alsatians of 1870, putting Bavarians or Prussians in their place, the French claims could have died out.

German claims to the territories east of the Oder–Neisse Line, which have become Russian or Polish, still persist, but one must consider the future. Although the refugees still claim the country of their ancestors, which they had to leave nineteen years ago, their children, who hardly knew the old country, are less interested in it; many prefer to remain in West Germany rather than return. The numerous and prolific Poles who have settled in East Germany will leave little room for Germans there in a few years. A new exchange of populations hardly appears possible, since the German as well as the Polish economy would be upset by it. West Germany could not easily do without the ten million men it has absorbed.

If we are surprised by the relative facility with which the operation has been effected, we must observe that migrations of peoples no longer encounter the same obstacles as they did formerly. Means of transportation are faster and more numerous. People are more accustomed to travel and leave their countries more easily; formerly, the vast majority of the population was rural, while it is now urban and working class. In an already overpopulated country, lands could not have been found for the masses of peasant refugees, but it was possible to build houses, factories, and offices for them and thus insure their being employed.

143

However we may judge the new German territorial status, all these reasons lead us to think that it may be of long duration. There are other reasons connected with the balance, or rather, the unbalance of forces between Germany and eastern Europe. It is understandable, however, that the Germans will maintain their claim on what they have lost, even if it must be platonic. Irredentism is the law of all peoples, even when only a tiny territory is concerned, and it would be illogical to think that it will not be applied to such a vast loss as that of eastern Germany. In the treaty (if one is ever signed) which settles the peace of Germany, would it be possible to insert a formula permitting the German people not to relinquish their claims formally, although they would bow before the facts?

This body of facts, if the German people considers its past and the territorial variations it has experienced, must give it reason for thinking that its history is not very satisfying. Are there many peoples who have so poorly managed their domain, trying to enlarge it and seeing it shrink and divide on so many occasions, only to find at the end of a period of fluctuation, that it has attained its maximum populations at the same time it has attained its minimum extent?

Such a phenomenon must have complex causes and all easy explanations should be rejected. The Germans, it is said, were always a restless, encumbering people, struggling to encroach on others, and they now have only what they deserve. History is not so simple. Let us not forget its hazards—without Hitler, Germany would not be what it is today, and it would also be different, if there had been no Bismarck, or if

Emperor Frederick, the father of William II, had not died after reigning only a few months.

It has been claimed that a policy which tried to maintain the division of Germany was the wisest one, and that it should have been pursued. Even if we admit that this was possible (but it is something which has not been proved, since all peoples instinctively seek their unity), this division stirred up multiple and contradictory ambitions, which conflicted with each other and pushed in all directions at once. Wouldn't a Germany containing all the Germans but limited to Germans alone have been less dangerous than the one which allowed its western marches to slip from it as it expanded over Burgundy, Italy, and Spain, which later on split into two empires, sought to rule over little Slav peoples, and finally attacked the largest one? How could such a people, which had the feeling of a community of language and culture, but not of a common destiny or of a common history, which had never seen itself drawn on a map with defined contours, not have been ready to participate in adventure?

The German people and other peoples as well may ask themselves if these adventures have come to an end.

[80]In 1918, Germany had lost 70,000 sq. km. and 6.5 million inhabitants.

[81]1959 census.

[82]See the chapter above, "The Franco–German Empire."

[83]In 1921, plebiscites in two Austrian provinces, Tyrol and Salzburg, gave more than ninety-eight per cent majorities in favor of *Anschluss.* Plebiscites scheduled for the other provinces were then forbidden by the Allies.

145

CHAPTER 14

Living Space?

ARE we to infer from the variations in Germany's situation, from this swing of the pendulum which has gone from a maximum to a minimum of political power and of territorial extent, that new changes are in the making? That this Germany which has retained its human potential and re-established its economy will try fatally to extend its borders? That it will persevere all the more along this path because German space has been so greatly reduced after the two wars?

Yet we must also ask whether or not Germany has really always sought to increase its living space, particularly towards the east and the south, towards Russia and the other Slavic countries, as Hitler intended to do. One hears it said that the early Germans probably invaded the west and the south of

Europe because they were too numerous, therefore because they lacked living space; or also because they were driven along by other peoples who had come from the east. The causes of the big invasions remain subject to discussion and are still being discussed. We observe, nevertheless, (1) that most of the Germanic peoples must have remained in Germany, since they were able to form a powerful kingdom there after the division of Charlemagne's empire, this kingdom was at first stronger than that of the Franks in the west, otherwise known as France; (2) that the invaders coming from Asia, the Huns, for example, far from driving the Germans ahead of them, were stopped by them either in Germany or in France and retreated. They could not have been very numerous and were engaged in incursions rather than in conquests. Later the Asiatic shock was absorbed principally by the Russians, located east of Germany; for many centuries they were under the yoke of the Tartars before they went into Asia and advanced all the way to the Pacific.

After Charlemagne, the Germans progressed by encroaching upon the Slavs in two directions. To the north, they occupied the strip of land between the Elbe and the Oder.[84] The Adriatic regions inhabited by the Croats and Slovenes would become a dependency of the Hapsburgs, who also became kings of Bohemia. In the north, the march forward was stopped by the thirteenth century, when the Germans met Polish resistance. Five hundred years elapsed before the next operation eliminated Poland, dividing it among Austria, Prussia, and Russia. This was not specifically a German undertaking; it was Russia who awarded herself the largest share of the destroyed Slav kingdom.

147

It follows that the so-called age-old struggle between Germans and Slavs is a formula which must be considered skeptically. Germany fought with the small peripheral Slavic peoples but she did not fight with the big Slavic people, the Russians, until the end of the nineteenth century. The latter encroached on her own "Slavic brethren" quite as much as Germany did. Was it to defend them or dominate them that Russia finally fought Germany? In the First World War one might be hesitant in deciding; after the Second, one observes that the Slavic peoples are all under Soviet Russian control.[85]

Hitler, critical of past German policy, reproached it for having moved in directions other than eastward. Even a superficial glance at the history of his country should have shown him that as soon as the western empire failed, German expansion did an about face to the east. Perhaps it was already too late. At the time of the big invasions, the absence of organized states in eastern Europe and the semi-nomadic character of the peoples scattered through the region would have permitted the Germans to expand there more easily than they could five or six centuries later. But in order to have all the chances on their side, shouldn't they have undertaken it still earlier, before the big invasions? In other words, these invasions should never have taken place, and this drive to the west and south should have been directed to the east. It is true that some migrations did move in that direction. In the second century A.D., the Goths, coming from the shores of the Baltic, had moved onto the shores of the Black Sea, driving out the Scyths and founding a kingdom which extended from the Carpathians to the Dnieper, or over

the present-day Ukraine. Defeated by the Huns, the Goths
fell back to the west, occupying the Danube basin, then Italy,
finally southern France, Spain, and North Africa. Burgunds
and Franks also established themselves in France, the Lom-
bards in the Po Valley, while the Angles and Saxons invaded
England; the latter were the only ones to succeed in founding
a predominantly German state. The others, in driving west
and south, were slowly absorbed by the peoples of older civi-
lizations, who were apparently more numerous.

If these Germanic tribes had stopped at the Rhine and
the Alps, would they not have been able to form a mass capable of holding the center and the southeast of Europe, from
the North Sea to the Black Sea? The Germans must then have
been stronger than the Slavs, whom they would have forced
to remain in the north of Russia. They had nothing to fear
from Rome, which was on the defensive. In the course of a
few centuries they could have set up the largest European
state of the time, three or four times larger than the empire
of William II. That would have been, it seems, a possible destiny for Germany after the conquest of Gaul by Caesar; nevertheless, rather than consolidate their positions in central
Europe, rather than extend them to the east, the Germans
began to clash with the Roman Empire, over which they
would soon flow in a great wave, but which resulted in no
methodical conquest; it was a rush of peoples, acting separately, each on its own account and often one against the
other. For a moment, one might think that the Franks, having
put a great empire together, would reign over a part of
Europe, including the west and Germania, but their empire
fell apart.

149

Such were the opportunities which were wasted by the Germans, although not by Germany, since it did not yet exist as an organized and united nation. They were probably, during the first centuries of the Christian era, the strongest people in Europe, in warlike qualities as well as in numbers. They were unable to profit from their advantages. Large states such as France and England were established around them, and were partly animated by German blood. The Slavs multiplied, forming one big and several smaller states. As it happens with most lost opportunities, these were lost forever. Twenty centuries after Caesar, in the time of Hitler, a people like the Russians, who had become more numerous than the Germans, and who had the largest and one of the most powerful states in the world, could not give up its place to Germany.

The Germans, moreover, long before Hitler, had understood this, hence the long friendship between Russia on the one hand and Prussia and Austria on the other. They fought as allies against Napoleon; the two German states abstained from the Crimean War. Two years after the war of 1870, William I and Francis Joseph concluded with the czar the so-called League of the Three Emperors. It would be short-lived, for Russia and Austria–Hungary would quarrel over their influence on the small Slavic peoples and Bismarck would support the latter. He had never had any designs on the living space which lay to the south and east of the new German Empire. As long as he remained in power, Russia maintained good relations with Germany, and it was because of her Austro–Hungarian ally that Germany had to enter a war disastrous to all three; an absurd war, in which Germany supported a tottering empire and Austria–Hungary and Russia

150

fought for little nations which would free themselves from both, although for only a short time.

In spite of everything which had happened, the traditional German–Russian friendship revived after the war. Relations were excellent, as the treaties of Rapallo and Berlin show, between the Soviet Republic and the Weimar Republic, the heirs of the two conquered empires. Until the advent of Hitler, one could not find a single anti-Russian note in the German press, whether of the right or the extreme left. Relations remained correct with Prague, with Belgrade; they were a little cool with Warsaw, but only because of the corridor. Between the two wars, the Germans never regretted the other territories which had been ceded to Poland. As citizens of Prussia, the Poles had been difficult, and there was no sorrow at separating from them.

In short it may be said that the only German–Slav quarrel after the war of 1914–1918 was over the Danzig Corridor.[86] It was not, moreover, so burning a question that it required immediate solution. Large and small Germans and Slavs could live henceforth on good terms, and a clever policy by Germany could have brought about a rapprochement. It took Hitler to reverse the situation, when he proclaimed, in the name of "living space," the submission, crushing, or expropriation of all the Slavic peoples, from the largest to the smallest.

In trying to impose German domination on them, he brought them under Soviet domination and succeeded in setting them up as a solid bloc against Germany. Nothing like it had ever been done in the past. Germany now finds herself in a difficult position in reference to the Slavic world. It is

151

no longer a matter of conquering or subjugating this world; it is part of a bloc which, extending to the ends of Asia, is infinitely more powerful than Germany. Even peaceful coexistence is difficult, for this Slav world is filled with mistrust and hatred for Germany. Will Germany ever be able to recover the vast territories she has lost, from which Russia and Poland have driven ten million inhabitants in order to replace them with their own?

There is no question that cities of 600 thousand inhabitants, like Breslau, for example, were completely German in 1949, that the population of these eastern territories, although they were Polish a few hundred years ago, had been Germanized for a long time, that they produced great philosophers like Kant and Schopenhauer, writers like Hoffman and Gerhart Hauptmann. Moreover, in driving out practically the whole of this population, the Poles openly recognized the fact that it was not theirs. But what weight do such facts have before the superiority of military might? The annexation of the territories lying beyond the Oder–Neisse Line to the U.S.S.R. and to Poland was done by Soviet will. On Moscow's part, this was an astute political act, intended to bind Poland irreparably to her. Although this people is both anti-Russian and anti-communist, it cannot abandon an ally which guarantees it such a vast increase in its territory. The U.S.S.R. will not abandon Poland for Germany, either, for the former is a safer ally than the latter. Germany, even if she should go communist, is too strong to be a satellite like the others.

However, doesn't interest in the lost provinces fade into the background when recovery of the Soviet occupation zone, extending to the center of Germany, is meeting with the greatest difficulties? One might have thought at first, after the Postsdam Agreement, that the occupation was temporary, that Dresden and Leipzig, Berlin, and Weimar would soon come back to Germany. Today, after the creation of the German Democratic Republic solidly allied to Moscow, after Khrushchev's repeated statements that this state is definitely part of the Soviet bloc, all Germans wonder about the chances for unification. That is another operation which, under present circumstances, could not be carried out except by force of arms, and force is not on the western side. The least we can say is that the matter appears to have been put off to the distant future.

This situation seems to deny Germany not only any claim to an increase in living space, but any claims that she could consider legitimate. Today and in the foreseeable future, she has no chance of satisfying them; one can always speculate about unexpected, exceptional events—but these cannot be taken into reasonable calculations.

If a policy of "living space" is no longer possible in the present, the Germans know it better than anyone else. It develops from all their history that they had scarcely established the policy before Hitler's time, and that their expansion moves stemmed from quite different causes.[87] In a situation which was more favorable than the present one, this policy was a failure. Henceforth, however, the enormous communist bloc which stretches to the limits of Asia will build an impenetrable wall against German undertakings.

For countries which appear overpopulated, there are means of subsistence other than the conquest of territories.

153

Since 1945, West Germany, despite the enormous influx of refugees, has shown that by hard work, by increasing its industrial and agricultural production, it could live and raise its standard of living. Isn't it furnishing a flagrant contradiction to the Hitler theories? Certainly peoples who can spread out over a large area, as those of the United States and the U.S.S.R. have done, are more favored than those who remain locked inside a small land. But the latter are more numerous, and if world population continues to grow at the current rate, the day will come when all will be equal in population. Their fate will be different only insofar as they prove to be more or less laborious and industrious, in exploiting their resources. In this respect, Germany is in the first rank; by giving up her errors, she thus has nothing to fear from the future.

[84]They went a little way beyond this river at a point near its mouth. On the right bank of the Vistula they occupied East Prussia, which became a German island in Slav territory.

[85]A question mark may be added for Yugoslavia. Nevertheless, she would not have her privileged position if she were not communist, therefore dependent on Moscow to a certain extent.

[86]The quarrel with Czechoslovakia over the Sudetens would be stirred up by Hitlerian propaganda. The matter never came up during the Weimar Republic.

[87]As is the case with most of the annexations carried out by other nations, those of the German princes stemmed from the ambition proper to all monarchs as well as from many other causes. In Bohemia, Frederick I of Austria was elected king by the states of that country and was also recognized as the king of Croatia. Thus two Slavic countries came under the Hapsburg Empire.

We must not forget, either, that until quite recent times, European countries were not over-populated and could not feel the need of "living space." This idea of "living space" is essentially modern.

154

CHAPTER 15

What is Militarism?

ONE reason for fearing Germany, a reason we cite freely, is "German militarism." Unlike "living space," this is no recent theory; militarism is supposed to be as old as the German people and in reality it is as old as the world itself. It is true, of course, that it can be seen in the ancient Germans. Later, one would have to say that war was the national industry of Prussia, although Prussia was not the same thing as Germany. Would it then always be necessary to fear wars that Germans might wage, even without a reason, for their own pleasure, as it were?

Militarism is found in the ancient world and even in primitive societies. Our distant ancestors were always at war, and among them the man of war held the first rank. It was he who commanded and who received public esteem and honors. Apparently, then, the characteristics of militarism are (1) that it is a phenomenon occurring in warring societies; (2) that it reserves first place to the soldier. The two characteristics are closely linked; in a people which is often at war, the man of war is the most useful man, and where the man of war is preponderant, it is natural that war should often be undertaken. It is difficult to distinguish between cause and effect.

History teaches us that the ancient Greeks were militarists. Before the time of the rhetors, the bearer of helmet and sword reigned undisputed among them. Would a William II, a Goering, however militaristic they may have been, ever have sacrificed their own daughter in order to be able to leave for combat a few days earlier, as Agamemnon did? In the Roman republic a statesman counted for nothing if he was not at the same time a general and a conqueror. The word emperor comes after all from *imperator,* "commander in chief." In feudal society and in the modern world which followed, militarism was the rule. The dominant nobility was originally the class of the warriors and could not have any profession other than that of arms without losing its status as nobility. In France, up to the Revolution, it was on its role as defender of the realm that it would base its privileges. Under Louis XIV, what were the architects of Versailles, the writers of genius, the bourgeois ministers like Colbert, beside the head of the army, who was always a nobleman? And what nobleman, bearing a great name, did not aspire to be commander of the armies? The militarism of that age is hidden from us by the brilliance of the court, its luxury, its festivals, and its prestige which spread beyond Paris, even beyond France. But the big concern of the king was not the plays of Molière nor the constructions of Mansart—it was his wars, his victories, his conquests, which courtiers, poets, and preachers vied with one another to honor. Who can say that the France of Louis XIV was not militaristic?

Napoleon's France was necessarily militaristic. When a victorious soldier dominates France, how would the military man's prestige not be the greatest? With the famous formula, "Each man has a marshal's baton in his cartridge-pouch," with young generals like Hoche, Moreau, and Bonaparte, the army became the finest of careers. Can democracy, which makes a soldier of every able-bodied man, and which places the highest ratings within reach of the brave, without distinction according to one's origin, oppose militarism? Although conscription does not necessarily imply militarism, it does accentuate certain of its defects; introduced little by little to all peoples, it will make wars more costly and longer. Those who, like the English, keep a professional army will be the least militaristic, despite appearances which seem to show that the professional soldier is the accomplice of a military dictatorship. The British army was never a privileged class, but an instrument in the hands of a ruling class formed of gentlemen farmers and merchants, who remained peacefully in their island, sending their soldiers out to fight when they deemed it useful.

What, then, is militarism? It might be appropriate to define accurately this term which everyone uses without knowing what it means. Is militarism confused with the warlike spirit, or with imperialism? Or are they engendered by it? Nothing is less certain. It can be said of the constitution of Sparta that it was militaristic, but that city was never big enough to carry out what we call imperialism. England, on the other hand, was an imperialistic but never a militaristic nation; Frederick II's Prussia, although it was militaristic, was too small to be imperialistic. Imperialism requires a certain degree of demographic, economic power, certain territorial dimensions which are the attributes of the big state. A small one can be militaristic, warlike, but it cannot be imperialistic; Russia has always been more imperialistic than militaristic; Franco's Spain is more militaristic than imperialistic.

Often what is meant by militarism is domination, or the predominance within a given state of a military clique, which does not necessarily have a warlike spirit. This predominance can be simply the social rank given to military men; it can also be their determining influence on politics. The military caste can be the army as a whole, but is probably the officer corps, or even a small number, such as the general staff, able to influence government leaders.

Germany, or rather Prussia, is held to be the typical militaristic nation of modern times. Here is how a German, Professor Siewerth,[88] defines the historical circumstances which produced this militarism:

> Without a strong military organization, Prussia, a poor country and one dangerously exposed to the east, would have succumbed to the pressures of its neighbors. But poverty in men and resources caused the army to suck up the energy, and so to speak, the substance of the country . . .

Prussia, unlike west and south Germany, had almost no urban civilization or any democratic tradition. The insignificance of the (Protestant) Church directly subordinated to the Crown, became disastrous for it, while in the countries of the west, the military machine was much larger but was counterbalanced by the structure of the Catholic Church and the vitality of the cities.

The organizing genius of the kings of Prussia, and the strategic power of Frederick II associated, somewhat romantically, the army and the king's person.

An important role is to be attributed to the meticulous seriousness of the Saxons, to the combative tradition of a land of colonists, finally to the mixture of Saxon dynamism and the malleability of the colonized Slavs.

The Napoleonic wars gave an almost religious and national consecration to militarism . . .

German unity, after the failure of the Parliament of Frankfort, was achieved by the force of arms, which implied again a very strong moral support in favor of the military factor . . .

The Reich, composed of different Laender with different feelings, was necessarily subordinated to the army, and the army's huge organization became the best agent of propaganda and of national unity.

One must realize the implication of a hundred years of military successes. From 1813 to 1914, the Prussian army, during five wars which were often long ones, suffered no defeat except that at Ligny. Such successes resulted in an extraordinary justification, so that it was psychologically impossible for the Germans not to esteem their army. The French attitude toward the successes of Napoleon was no different and that of the English toward their invincible navy was the same.

The army represented moreover, the best support of the Crown in its struggle with liberalism and socialism. In the midst of revolutionary tendencies it was, so to speak, the conservative element which insured the prodigious development of the state and of the economy.

This historical explanation of Prussian militarism apparently covers the essential points: the country's geographic situation, the racial composition of the early Prussians, the lack of an urban civilization in a colonized country which had been taken over little by little from a peasant population, the role played by sovereigns like Frederick William I, the "sergeant-king" and Frederick II, the great captain, the place taken by Prussia in 1813 in the war of "liberation" against Napoleon, and in the war of 1870.

The persistance of militarism in Prussia and its disappearance in France can be explained by the fact that in France the imperial regime had fallen, whereas the Prussian royalty, raised to empire status, saw its authority grow after it had wrought a kind of German unity. The role of the army as supporter of the crown against socialism and liberalism in the Germany of William II could probably be compared to that attributed in the Third Republic to the French army, called "reactionary" up to the time of the Dreyfus affair. The prestige of the uniform and of the military hierarchy, greater in Germany than in France, the comradeship among soldiers to which Germans are highly sensitive, also contributed to the strengthening of militarism, at first in Prussia, then throughout Germany.

There is no point in insisting on the secondary aspects of Prussian militarism, striking as they may be—the haughty bearing and pretentiousness of the officer, very pronounced in William II's army, but attenuated in the Weimar Reichswehr and in Hitler's Wehrmacht—the pride of the civilian made lieutenant in the reserve—and finally the social rank held by the army. A more important point would be the political influence of military men. It was under William II and during the Weimar Republic that this was most marked; it was less evident with Bismarck and Hitler. Military men grow all the stronger as civilians grow weaker. Bismarck had excellent relations with the army chiefs. Sometimes he had to give in to them, for example, on the conditions of the Treaty of Frankfort,[89] but in peacetime he did not tolerate their intervening in his policy. Although the General Staff had the ear of William II (less than did Admiral von Tirpitz), the Kaiser had only a military chancellor, General Caprivi, an unimportant man. The others were civilians, diplomats, or high-level government employees, like Bülow or Bethmann-Hollweg. It isn't easy to estimate what share each had in the major decisions the Kaiser had to make. But the world was struck by something "militaristic" which was sensed in his words, bearing and habits, although William II was not a real military man like Frederick.

Paradoxical as it may appear at first blush, it was under the Weimar Republic that the influence of the army reached its highest point. The founders of the republic committed a serious error at the beginning—they could not, as the communists in Russia had done, insure to themselves an army

161

devoted to the new regime.[90] They allowed it to fall into the hands of the generals and the cadres of the old regime; at its head was a remarkable organizer, von Seekt, and later, a politician-general, von Schleicher, who engaged in secret intrigues and was the last head of the government before Hitler.

Various circumstances combined to give to the Reichswehr of the Versailles Treaty an importance which it did not merit, for it included (theoretically, at least) only a hundred thousand men. First there was the election of Hindenburg, the most popular soldier of the war, as president of the Reich, with the extended powers which he would abuse—and later, the very restrictions which the treaty had imposed on this army and which were circumvented insofar as possible and with general complicity. If a big army can be dangerous, an army placed in the position of the sacrificed child, the unjustly treated child, is equally dangerous. It enjoys the prejudice people have in its favor, and the most ardent anti-militarists are willing to forgive it anything. If it sets up a barely secret system for increasing the prescribed numbers of troops, everyone closes his eyes. If it sends aviators to Russia for training, what a good trick played on the Allies! The minister asks for a "vest-pocket battleship"—who would dare refuse him?

The Reichswehr did not openly combat the Weimar Republic, but it did not give it the support it could and should have given. Political leaders scarcely dared give it orders, and the military chiefs sometimes used angry gestures. Before Hitler's rise to power, Chancellor von Schleicher could have the republicans and the socialists behind him, but still he capitulated before Hindenburg because of military discipline, which required that a general obey a marshal. If he had not, the army, by the same principle, would no doubt not have followed him. And he had to have the armies as well as the parties in order to succeed.

According to a legend which is rather widespread, particularly outside Germany, Hitler is supposed to have been a simple tool of the Wehrmacht; it is true that this army rallied to him easily at first, not foreseeing (no one did) the kind of regime he was going to establish. The military men thought they could take pride in the creation of powerful forces, which promised them enlistments and promotions. However, they would not be long in singing another tune—Hitler would treat their great chiefs as no other regime had ever dared to do.

He removed General von Blomberg, the minister of war, using his marriage as a pretext; next it was General von Fritsch, the commander in chief, removed as the result of a calumnious accusation by the Gestapo.[91] The whole army was outraged. Hitler was unperturbed; he removed from duty sixteen other generals who were hostile to national socialism.

All the documents published since the war prove that Hitler hated his generals. Considering himself a military genius, he often spurned their advice. It is well known that they were opposed to the occupation of the demilitarized zone of the Rhineland in 1936; they did not favor his undertakings against Czechoslovakia and Poland. His hatred became a veritable fury after the assassination plot of July 20, 1944; it was followed by a wholesale sacrifice of generals and colonels.

National socialism was dictatorial, totalitarian, and conquering. It was not really militaristic, if one understands by
that term a regime taking its power in the army. Hitler used
the army for his conquests, but his authority was not based
on it; it was based on the single party and on the police, which
formed the framework of the regime. It is not in the tradition
of military men to carry out the ignoble tasks which absolute
power required, and the Gestapo controlled the army as well
as the other institutions.

A dictator who never rose above the rank of corporal
could not but mistrust his generals, especially in wartime,
when their powers were almost unlimited. He said to himself that by taking recourse in the forces they commanded,
they could overthrow him and take his place. Those who revolted on July 20 would easily have done so if their plot had
been better prepared. Hitler knew it, and that is why he executed a ferocious vengeance upon them.

The reproach which might be made to the German military men, who for the most part were hostile to him personally
and to his regime, is that they did not use their privileged
position to take action against him. According to certain evidence which does not seem decisive, they may have been
on the verge of acting on the eve of Munich; the Allies' capitulation may have cut the ground from under them. On July
20, 1944, a series of unfortunate circumstances caused the
attempt to fail; the bomb did not strike the intended victim,
and most of the conspirators had shown themselves hesitant.
The grave wounds suffered by Rommel in Normandy three
days before, when he was about to ask an armistice for the

German armies of the west, put an end to this attempt which no doubt came too late.

The fact is that these military men, suspected of trying to dominate German policy, were so submissive to whatever government was in power that they dared not rise against it. They obeyed Hitler as they had the Kaiser and the Weimar Republic, which they had not supported, although they did not revolt against it. Discipline was so firmly anchored in their nature that they considered any avoidance of it to be sacrilege, and preferred to put up with an authority of which they disapproved rather than revolt against it.[92] There never has been any generals' uprising, and *coup d'état* or *pronunciamento* in Germany, no Napoleon or Boulanger, no Pétain or De Gaulle; civil power has never been fought for or seized by military men. Although Marshal Hindenburg became president of the Reich, it was as the result of a popular vote in conformity with the constitution.[93]

What leads one to believe in the influence of the military men in the national-socialist state is that there was a military element in the organization and in the very spirit of the regime. Like all military regimes, it was based on that rigorous discipline without which no army can subsist, but which does not appear necessary in a civil society.

The triumph of national socialism may have been faciltated by a certain disposition, both a habit and a frame of mind, which militarists had inculcated in the German people. From the barracks it had entered the school, had worked into this whole people, accentuating a natural bent for obedience, and making docile tools of them in a dictator's hands. Wasn't

165

the civilians, who in William II's time had imitated the military and bowed to it as he did to the Kaiser as the supreme commander of the army, ready to bow before a chief a thousand times more authoritarian than the emperor, and who was simply exaggerating the former system? Was not national socialism the direct product of German militarism, forcing the tendencies it had cultivated and carrying into every field the methods which had been proper to it? If militarism, before Hitler, had developed and maintained a strong discipline everywhere, the Nazi leader tightened this discipline to the maximum and concentrated authority in the single party of which he was the head. Thus the excess of power of the army, infinitely multiplied, overflowed into all the professions, all the classes and milieux, and the sergeant's kick in the draftee's behind led to the gas chamber.

National socialism could be defined as militarism carried to the absurd, to the monstrous. We might see a certain logic in this evolution, but logic does not always dominate policy. It's a long way from Frederick and William II to Hitler, and we see that all peoples subjected to totalitarian regimes, whether Communist or Fascist, show the same obedience, not to say the same servility, as the Germans did under Hitler. With all human beings, don't extremely swift and brutal punishments put an end to all desire for independence?

Can military men still play a great role in the modern state outside of the one proper to them, which is to defend the nation? Let us omit countries with a special mentality, such as those of Latin America and the Near East, where generals, even colonels, seize power after a *coup d'état*. Regimes which result from such revolutions are not properly speaking militaristic, but dictatorial, with the defects of dictatorships, including the penchant for military adventures. This characteristic is also found in dictatorships ruled by civilians, notably in young nations, exalted by the feeling of newly won independence and eager to assert themselves, such as China; and even in non-dictatorial countries obliged to defend themselves against a stronger enemy, as is the case of Israel. Let us note that the Chinese and the Israelites[94] have always been considered particularly peaceful peoples. Doesn't their example prove that the warlike spirit, if not militarism, can move from one people to another?

In the western nations which have been fighting with each other for fifteen hundred years, the prestige of the army is no longer great enough for a government or the head of a state, even a militaristic state, to be able to influence men's thinking in favor of war and to declare it thoughtlessly. An army is thought of today as a costly and dangerous tool to be handled with care. It has an inherent strength which can drive a nation to catastrophe. Armies can be a means of avoiding war, of defending oneself if war breaks out, but they may also be a cause of war; they are at one and the same time a good and an evil, and we realize today that in order to prevent them from causing misfortune, we must be careful not to play with them, not to swell their prestige, not to make too big a place for them in our society, as this would allow them to encroach upon the activities of peace.

A people like the Germans, who have undergone two unprecedented defeats in less than thirty years, are as much aware of this as others, and perhaps more. The hostility the Germans have shown toward all rearmament even reveals a fear of the military apparatus which might be considered abnormal, in view of the fact that Germany's geographic location and political situation makes her one of Europe's most exposed countries. Perhaps this is the civilian's inferiority complex; during the first German republic he was unable to put the military in its place and he now sees no other solution except to suppress it.

This frame of mind, emerging just after the war, has recently become attenuated. The social-democrats who had advocated the *ohne mich* (count me out) formula are openly rallying to national defense. An army reform intended to make of the soldier a civilian in uniform, and which was carried so far that draftees have been known to complain about the softness of discipline, seems to be giving way to a more normal conception of the people under arms. Profound and long-lasting and anti-militarism might have made Gernamy incapable of fulfilling the task which await her, either in reuniting or in the defense of the Western world. It would be tragic if after having been militaristic when it should not have been, the German people should now reject the minimum of militarism necessary for survival.

Military leaders, as well as the most insignificant citizen will have to understand henceforth that the army is no longer anything more than a cog in the vast machine which must include the whole population in time of war, and in which the technician is more important than the professional soldier, in which the brilliance and the glory disappear in the terror of bombings, and the non-combattant may be more exposed than the soldier. They must not forget that quarrels between great nations are no longer justifiable (if they can ever be justified), except from the point of view of the large interests and the great passions which divide human kind. When the problem is that of learning what way of thinking, of living, and of organizing society will win over the other, what importance can the voice of a few military men have? Their authority in times still close to us was merely a surviving element of primitive times when the lives and property of unarmed men, women, and children was at the mercy of those who carried the sword. In today's world there is no longer any room for the soldier's rule, unless it is among less developed peoples.

Must we believe, despite the precautions which have been taken, that the presence of an army could influence Germany's domestic and foreign policy? A government, whatever it may be, does not behave in the same way when it has an army behind it as it does when there is no such support. Hasn't the most powerful army in the world weighed upon Soviet policy since the last war? Doesn't American policy feel the effects of having a huge navy, air force, and atomic weapons? Don't the Pentagon and the high command of the Atlantic army insure for the American army, even in peacetime, a greater influence than it had earlier in United States policy? In other countries, this influence stems from other causes. In France, a series of difficulties which struck the army in 1940, then in Indochina, and in Algeria, have provoked a sudden reaction within it, and we do not know what its results might have been, if a man whom the army respected had not contained them. Such episodes may remind civilians that even if the military obeys them, they must also take its feelings into account. Like all men, military men have their *esprit de corps* and their conception of national policy.

Today, however, there are few chances that militarism and military men will intervene in a declaration of war. They are too familiar with the possible, even probable results of armed conflict. No one is ignorant of the fact that a few H-bombs would suffice to annihilate Germany.[85] We must not be taken in by words or myths. Prussian militarism, although it was formerly real and was closely linked to the history of Prussia, belongs to the past as does the militarism of ancient Rome or of Napoleonic France. The state which gave birth to it no longer exists. It is not very likely that the present situation of Germany will permit the rebirth of a political system dominated by military men. Less unlikely might be the return to a more nationalistic policy than today's, but militarism and nationalism are not identical. Although nationalism can make use of military men, it is not necessarily their creation, and could almost dispense with them.

[88]Cf. *Documents*, May, 1949.

[89]At least he claimed that he was not in favor of the annexation of Metz and that it was imposed by the General Staff. It still remains to be seen if he did not attribute this responsibility to it in order to escape from it himself.

[90]The Red army was created six months after the communist take-over. Isn't it because of this army that they were able to remain in power?

[91]General von Fritsch was accused of homosexuality. No redress was offered him when it was proved that this was a case of error caused by a similarity of names.

[92]The controversy which arises every year in Germany over the anniversary of the 20th of July is revealing in this regard. Many generals and officers of all ranks stated that although they were opposed to Hitler and national socialism, they could not betray their oath to the head of the army. Colonel Stauffenberg, who delivered the bomb intended to kill Hitler, was himself haunted by these scruples, which were strengthened by his Catholic faith. His oath, for him, had a truly religious character.

[93]Moreover, Hindenburg was not voted in by plebiscite, as Napoleon III had been, but was elected by a relative majority over Chancellor Marx, of the Catholic center. He would no doubt not have been elected if the communists had withdrawn their candidates on the second ballot.

[94]Not the Israelis, who are Israelites holding a territory. This difference has been enough to change their character.

[95]Mr. Khrushchev has set the figure at eight.

CHAPTER 16

Two Different Nationalisms

NATIONALISM, like militarism, is old—a little less old than militarism, but the name itself is new.[96] There is occasionally an attempt to distinguish it from patriotism, with which it might tend to be confused. It might be defined as an accentuation of the national point of view, particularly in politics. And, of course, there is cultural nationalism, economic nationalism, etc.

At first glance nationalism would seem to be a natural tendency. It is found, not without some exaggeration, in the new nations. We talk of German nationalism, but what is one to think of the Arabs, the Chinese, the Indians, the Vietnamese, the natives of Ghana or Guinea? All an African tribe or an Asiatic principality has to do today is to wave the flag of nationalism, and people all over the world who call themselves anti-nationalists will praise it to the skies.

172

Accentuation of the national point of view leads the inhabitants of one nation to oppose those of another or of several others. Nationalism easily becomes provocative and aggressive. When does it pass the line of demarcation on this side of which it may be considered normal, on the other side of which it enters the zone of aggressiveness? People never agree on this. Two hostile peoples will reproach each other for their nationalism; no one can say who is right and who is wrong, and generally, both are right and wrong simultaneously. And so it happens that the French have always characterized German nationalism as intolerable, and the Germans have been equally critical of French nationalism; each sees his neighbor's nationalism without seeing his own. In France, the first to adopt the word and to appeal to it were such writers as Barrès and Maurras. They attributed to it a sovereign virtue which their opponents would not grant it. These opponents saw the French nationalists as reactionaries, along with the Pan-Germanists. Moreover, many of those who opposed nationalism in words revealed that they were as nationalistic in their feelings as the nationalists themselves. Such are the complications of politics and its vocabulary. Clearly, national or nationalist policy (there is only a shade of difference in meaning between the two adjectives)[97] existed long before it was named. Any constituted, organized state follows a nationalist policy, even if it is not a true nation. Were the Romans nationalists? In other words, is a people which attains imperial dimensions, swallowing up many other peoples in the process, still nationalist? The question is debatable. Contemporary examples seem to indicate that it is possible. Big new states, such as India, or Indonesia, formed of dozens of peoples with as many languages, are no less nationalist than the states formed by a single people. On the other hand, there is an Arab nationalism which crosses over the boundaries of states.

We shall limit our discussion to German and French nationalisms, the nationalisms of two peoples who were once united, but who have been separated since the time of Charlemagne's grandsons. The striking thing here is that these two nationalisms differ from their very beginnings, and for historical reasons.

French royalty, having fought successfully against the feudal lords, reigned in the true sense of the word over France at the very time when the German emperors, powerful at first, were losing all their power inside their own empire. It followed that in France nationalism was identified early with loyalty to the king—to be French or to be the subject of the king of France were one and the same thing. It cannot be said that the same was true of Germany, where a subject of the emperor belonged at the same time to other sovereigns who still retained great power. On the other hand, this emperor, who had long reigned, at least as suzerain, over northern Italy and southeastern France, had numerous subjects who were not Germans. Anyone living in Brussels or in Madrid could recognize the imperial sovereignty, but he did not feel that he was German. To know to what nation he did belong, we should have to seek another criterion, that of his language.

Much later it would be said that the thinkers of the eighteenth century founded German nationalism on the German language. Is this correct? Doesn't this circumstance correspond rather to historical necessity? A people in whom political authority remained for centuries so complex, and so divided, while other peoples of western Europe, the French, Spanish, English, were becoming great national unities, could recognize itself only by its linguistic unity. This unity, despite the multiplicity of dialects which long existed, did constitute a powerful bond, particularly since the common tongue did not only allow the Germans to communicate with each other, but also served as the basis for a great literature. The German translation of the Bible by Luther was a national event which had no equivalent in any other country.

The difference in origin and essence between the German and French nationalisms explains the fact that for centuries there was no truly *national* opposition between the two peoples, whereas there was between the French and the English, for example, during the Hundred Years' War. When the troops of Charles V fought in Provence or in Champagne, people did not speak of the "Germans," but of the "imperials" —the mercenaries of the Hapsburgs. They might be Czechs, Hungarians, Croats, Belgians, or Spaniards as well as Germans. There were also Germans, Rhinelanders, Saxons, Bavarians, and Prussians who did not fight against France at that time. It was basically a matter of dynastic rivalry rather than one of national conflict, and again, this is what explains the fact that an anti-Hapsburg, but not anti-German nationalism appeared a little later in France, when an anti-French nationalism arose in Germany. The same difference persisted: German nationalism could be anti-French, since France was identified with its monarch; French nationalism could not be anti-German, since there was no Germany, but an emperor without authority over the major part of Germany, and who owed the essential part of his power to non-Germanic peoples.

This difference would lead to strange confusions. In the eighteenth century, the French would applaud the victory of a German, the king of Prussia, over their own army—hadn't this same king of Prussia defeated the Austrians, the Hapsburgs, France's enemies? In Germany, however, the victory at Rossbach stirred up enthusiasm which largely overflowed Prussia's structure and took on an anti-French character, since France was the defeated power. Up to the Revolution, the French would be pro-Prussian, out of hatred for the Hapsburgs, and without suspecting that Prussia would one day be the rallying point for the Germans against them.

It would take the wars of the Revolution and the empire for the two nationalisms to crystalize and face each other. The French nationalism assumed an explosive force that it had been unable to have under royalty, by the fact that the nation was now assimiliated to the people and was no longer personified by the monarch, and by the fact that the people were called to arms to "carry liberty" beyond their borders.

In 1815, the conflict of these two nationalisms began, a conflict of two peoples—it was not a conflict of two states, since there was no single Germany. There was, however, a German national awareness; this had not been the case earlier. From time to time bursts of public opinion set French and

176

Germans against each other. They threw up their nationalism to each other, and their territorial claims; for the Germans, Alsace, for the French, the left bank of the Rhine—until the clash occurred which would result in the victory of Germany and in the creation of a great German state. From that time on, the clash of the two nationalisms would be at the same time the clash of two peoples and two governments. The nationalism of the peoples would strengthen the nationalism of the governments and vice versa. On both sides a nationalist policy caused nationalist feeling to increase, but we may also say that nationalist feeling inspired the policy. Policy and feeling are inseparable. Bismarck justified his policy by France's desire for revenge, while the French statesmen justified their anti-German alliances by the threat of a Germanic aggression. Nationalism became a vicious circle from which no one could escape.

But the two nationalisms would then differentiate themselves in still another way. The French nationalism, of long standing, was essentially conservative. If it had any claim to make it was at the most that of Alsace–Lorraine. And this claim was moreover softened by time and would have become purely academic if a war due to other reasons had not broken out in 1914.

German nationalism rapidly adapted to circumstances. Bismarck, once he had attained his first objective, which was German unity, could rest on his laurels. After him, however, this nationalism became a weight too heavy to be manipulated by a weak emperor; it was the weight of a great people whose demographic, economic, and military power went on growing. This power may have gone to the Kaiser's head; it did require actions, but they should have been efficient without being provocative. The Kaiser sensed this but did little more than make speeches and gestures which disturbed the world, and issue incoherent formulae. He was neither a soldier nor a conqueror; as conquests he had offered his people only Kiaochow and the Congo "duck bill." He assumed a negative attitude at the two Hague conferences, allowed the Russian and British alliances to slip from his hands, and picked a bad quarrel in Morocco. He lacked psychology and imagination.

From a nationalism founded on real power like that of Germany, a great politician could have drawn something better than a world war and a defeat. Couldn't such power have been used without recourse to arms? Germany was in a better position than anyone else to accept the beginning of disarmament, and this would have reduced tensions in the European atmosphere. Her position in international trade was excellent and could be improved; although it was difficult for her to enlarge her colonial domain (she was a late comer to the dividing up of Africa), she could exploit fully colonies which were valuable. Many concessions would have been made to a moderate and prudent Germany, but people bristled against the arrogant and threatening Germany.

It does not often happen that a conquered people, conquered in the way the Germans had been, creates a crisis of nationalism like that of Germany between the two world wars. After such clashes people generally incline toward pacifism; the German nationalists, however, had the impression of having been frustrated, because during the war they had sensed in their country that same strength which they had felt in peacetime. The Allies had thought to show them that a nation, however strong, does not resist a superior coalition. But the demonstration was not understood, the victory was not enough; no doubt a victory policy was needed, and the policy of the conquerors was awkward and soft.

As for French nationalism, which had been irritable just after the war, it dropped to zero in a few years, to the critical point at which a people stops being combative, where it no longer has even the elementary reflexes of the instinct of self-preservation. Faced with a dynamic, expansive German nationalism, France, turning inward, watched apathetically the tumultuous motions of her neighbor, as if she herself were not a nation, but a collection of little people, led by little politicians and little habits. The result was to be the "phony war" and the disaster of 1940.

Two doctrinary peoples

Before and after World War I, nationalist doctrines flourished in France and in Germany. They were a complement of politics and of the national feeling, a complement which wasn't indispensable but which was characteristic of the two peoples. Others, like the English, always nationalistic by instinct, did not feel this need to adorn their policy with theories. The interplay of ideas and the mania for justifying acts by words is apparently a Franco–German specialty.

However different they may have been, the French and German theoreticians of nationalism often extended a hand to each other. The initiator of racism was Gobineau, whose *Essay on the Inequality of the Human Races* dates from 1854. His theories had less repercussion in France than in Germany, where they influenced Pan-Germanism, not to be confused with racism, although it has several points in common with it.

Pan-Germanism would preach the rallying of all Germans, even of all the Teutonic strains, would try to bring into a great German state all those who had been separated from it for centuries. Theoretically, this idea was capable of winning support; the Pan-Germanists' mistake was that it came late. Most of the Germanic groups separated from Germany, such as Switzerland, Holland, Flanders, had created a separate existence and no longer desired to return to the main trunk from which they had sprung.[98] Although history, or rather simply the past, may explain Pan-Germanism to a certain extent, it does not justify it. Pan-Germanism closed its eyes to an evolution which would no longer allow the clock to be turned backwards without upsetting Europe.

"Living space" and racism would give national socialist ambitions reasons which were both vaguer and more convenient. These two theories support and complement each other. To enlarge a country like Germany effectively, it wasn't enough to annex neighboring territories—they must be emptied of their populations, on the pretext that they were of an inferior race, and room had to be made for Germans. Hitler, had he been victorious, would not have hesitated to push back fifty million Poles and Russians. As for the Jews, he adopted pure and simple liquidation. In a case of this kind, the theory is no mere adjuvant of the policy; it becomes its indispensable vehicle. The policy needs it to justify acts which are contrary to all customs and rules which are admitted in the civilized world. Could Hitler have attacked Poland and Russia if he had not at the very least persuaded his faithful that his aggressions were necessary to enlarge Germany? He had exposed the principles according to which he wanted to act in *Mein Kampf,* a book which was on every German's shelf.[99] Such use of doctrine constitutes real misuse. Not only is it contrary to the law of humanity, it also loses contact with the realities of power as well as with the ideas and feelings current in its time. In brutally opposing them, could it produce anything but catastrophe?

French nationalism is distinguished from German nationalism by its intellecutal origins and by its goals, which appear modest, compared to the excesses of Pan–Germanism and racism. They scarcely went further than the aims of political opinion. A century after the Revolution, the left bank of the Rhine appeared as nothing but a distant dream, in which the average Frenchman was losing interest and which attracted only a few who had a mania for the past. After 1918, Clémenceau opposed this annexation, and the attempts at the "Rhineland Republic" received no support from the French government. In 1945, no one took seriously the Ruhr separation proposal made by a French minister, Bidault, and the seizure of the Saar would be only temporary, since there would be no popular support for it.

Contrary to Germany, where nationalist theories were the product of a more or less adulterated science, France offered a nationalism which was under the protection of such good authors as Barrès and Maurras. They were not highly original, being inspired by the philosophers and historians of the preceding period, such as Taine, Renan, Le Play, and others. They wanted to bring into politics a point of view opposed to that of the eighteenth-century thinkers. Their point of view was not only nationalist, but also conservative and anti-democratic. They thought it was less a matter of enlarging the territory than it was of combating that universal reason which had become for a century the political gospel of France; they sought rather to root the individual in the national whole, to attach him to the soil of his native village and of his province, to strengthen his bonds with his compatriots. Attachment to tradition, to all that is permanent, materialistically or spiritually, the milieu, the climate, the landscape, the architectural and literary monuments, the religion and customs inherited from ancestors—it was all that which nationalism wanted to call back and consolidate. Nationalism held that these realities had been lost from sight since men had turned exclusively to the rational and abstract man.

Barrès, borrowing much from Taine, added the anti-German barb which Taine did not have; this tendency seems a little forced in this man from Lorraine, the compatriot of Victor Hugo and who, like him, had a certain open-mindedness toward Germany. More sincere and profound was the Germanophobia of Maurras, who was totally prejudiced against the Germanic world. For this Provençal, the Teuton was the pure barbarian, the *bête noire* par excellence, Satan in person. In his desire to establish the German as the opposite of all that was French and Latin, he constructed a Mediterranean France, heiress of Athens and Rome, a pure product of his imagination—as if the olive tree grew on the Puy-de-Dome or Montmartre! But France is an Atlantic country by its coastline, its rivers, its climate, its vegetation. Paris is one hundred sixty kilometers from the English Channel and six hundred from the Mediterranean, and the Latin sea for the French is nothing more than a resort area where they go for a change of scene and a sunburn. Although they got their language from Rome, aren't their ancestors Celto–Germans at least as much as they are Greco–Latins?

Although the theories of the French nationalists had nothing in common with Pan-Germanism and racism, we must not think of them as the absolute opposites of German nationalism or even of German thought, as their authors would have it. This thought had filled Barrès' master. Is his formula "the land and our dead," so different for the racist Darré's *Blut und Boden,* and is the order extolled by Maurras as the first requirement of any policy not the same as the essential rule of that Prussian tradition which the German nationalists wanted to incorporate in their system? Basically, the French nationalists admired the *Realpolitik* of Bismarck, so decried in France. A hidden fiber unites nationalists of all countries; they hate each other and feel irresistably attracted to each other.

Nationalism, right and left

In France there are also nationalists whom we may place on the left; they are perhaps the most anti-German. It must not be forgotten that the Revolutions gave more than a theory to French nationalism—it gave its whole expression, allowed it to expand and to become a conqueror. Its tradition always rises up again at the desired moment. When the parties which call themselves nationalistic felt defeated after the Dreyfus affair, one might have thought that French politics, moving down the anti-militarist incline, would evolve toward a pacifist socialism. Nationalism, however, took a turn to the left at that time and found itself at the head of France with the Jacobin Clémenceau. Today, Jacobinism, spread among the leftist parties from the radicals to the communists, perhaps no longer has the same strength, or the same resonance, but it remains capable of producing national explosions. This faculty of nationalism of adapting to all political tendencies is the essential point to be retained about nationalist doctrines, which are outmoded today and even unknown to the new generations. In Germany, as in France, nationalism was long the attribute of the parties of the right, but today, the communists, who are both chauvinists and universalists, are beating everyone on this ground. German Socialists, accused of national coolness under the Weimar Republic, are as nationalistic as the Christian Democrats. If they take power tomorrow, their policy may be more "national" than that of the European, Adenauer.[100]

Is nationalism retreating or being reborn?

Here we have returned to an essential political question, which is still the major question for both the present and the future: how are French and German nationalism going to behave when they are face to face? Since 1945 they have got

184

along rather well, much better than they did after the First World War. After a conflict in which France and Germany were both losers, the aspirations and feelings which feed nationalism seemed to have fallen to their lowest ebb. It would be too much to say that public opinion in the two countries, led in this direction by certain sensible and resolute men like Chancellor Adenauer, President Schuman, M. Monnet, and M. François–Poncet, has allowed itself to be persuaded. At least it has followed their lead with a more or less hesitant step. Nationalism, however, habitually sleeps with one eye open, and it would be a serious error indeed to believe it has disappeared simply because it has appeared to be relatively modest in recent years. If certain circumstances have made it drowsy, others can awaken it, especially if the intellectuals and the press, the great artisans of nationalism, begin to fan the flame. That is an eventuality for which we must be constantly prepared. We have defined nationalism as "the accentuation of the national viewpoint." So long as men live in national states, there will be times when this accentuation will be inevitable under the pressure of events. There are other times when, for the same reason, nationalism will be attenuated. If two neighboring peoples, habitually quick to quarrel with each other, desire better relations, they will have to observe attentively these changes in the situation and mood of the partner; they will have to refrain from throwing up their hands and crying scandal if one day this neighbor assumes attitudes more nationalistic than those of the day before. These changes in direction can be due to inevitable circumstances which we must try to understand in order to get along with them.

In today's German youth, aversion to nationalism is instinctive; it sees nationalism as bound up with Hitlerian imperialism. A large proportion of these young people would scarcely admit that the idea of the nation has any value at all. This may be a temporary frame of mind, a reaction against the mentality which led Germany to catastrophe, and it can only be softened with time, and give way to different, if not opposite views.

France, for several years, has been brought to a certain nationalism as she gathered up the remnants of her former empire;[101] the same thing may happen to Germany as she struggles for her unity. These are not conflicting objectives; they will be pursued separately, and although they may momentarily move the two peoples away from each other (no one can embrace everything at once, each one busies himself with what concerns him most closely), Germany and France will find each other again, once their immediate concerns have been removed.

As for the economic needs which motivate all peoples and put them into competition, they will be all the better coordinated between France and Germany because they will meet in an enlarged market, where all the European peoples will strive to do their best. On this ground there must be no rivals, but emulators. In this field as in the political field, we must tell ourselves that national tendencies, traditions, and interests will not be eliminated overnight; their highs and their lows must be accepted calmly and with understanding; we must not lose sight of the fact that we are dealing after all with aftereffects from the past. For peoples like the French and the Germans, the great era of nationalism, despite its possible resurgences, must come to an end. These people will not live, will not prosper, unless they give it up, except in critical moments, to the new nations, and unless common action and thought dictate their behavior.

[96]The words "nationalism" and "nationalist" do not appear in the Littré dictionary nor in the more recent Darmestetter dictionary. One finds them in the Grand Larousse with the note that they are "neologisms," and in two texts of Proudhon and Berlioz. The eighth and last edition of the Academy's dictionary defines nationalism as "a feeling which consists in exalting the national idea."

Was it Barrès who introduced it into France in current usage about 1892? "Nationalist" parties already existed in Hungary and Ireland.

[97]Machiavelli had said long before: "The country must always be saved, in honor or in infamy, but it must be saved." The English would express this in a more concise manner: "My country, right or wrong." These statements show how difficult it is to distinguish between the "nationalist" and the "national" point of view.

[98]See p. 180 *supra.*

[99]Which doesn't mean that every German had read it. There are even excellent reasons for believing that most had not, which seems regrettable. The passages explicated for school children were carefully selected.

[100]The Franco–German conflict has sometimes been presented, particularly since 1870, as a conflict of ideas; German political and philosophic thought, designated under the inaccurate term "Germanism," is contrasted with French thought; on one side, a current which, going back to Herder and running through Hegel and Nietzsche, produced the theoreticians of Pan-Germanism and racism; on the other side, the rationalism which flows from the philosophers of the eighteenth century and which is used as authority by French democracy.

It is useless to say that this is a simplistic view. Herder was no stranger to the humanitarian ideas of his century. Hegel produced Marx. Nietzsche, whose filiation of ideas goes back to Schopenhauer rather than to Hegel, fought Prussian militarism and wanted to be a European before being a German.

In France, since the nineteenth century, anti-revolutionary thought is hardly less important than that of the heirs of Voltaire and Rousseau. It is enough to mention such names as Joseph de Maistre, Bonald, Auguste Comte, Taine, Le Play, Renan, Gobineau, Georges Sorel, and Maurras, to note that the French are divided between the two tendencies.

The traditions which dictated Germany's policy, and men like Bismarck or William II, who directed it, had few points in common with German philosophy. In France, revolutionary tradition and ideas had a greater influence on policy, particularly in the field of home affairs. In international relations, these ideas sometimes pushed France toward pacifism, sometimes toward war, and in this area there was also the influence of a nationalist tradition as firmly anchored as that of Germany.

[101]Cf. *Le Monde,* November 5, 1954: "M. Bidault has certain points in common with his successor (M. Mendès–France): his nationalism."

La Figaro, January 22, 1957: "Incidentally, it was France which invented nationalism." (From an American's answer to Thierry Maulnier.)

CHAPTER 17

Responsibilities and Character

Is there a collective responsibility?

WE have acquired the habit of discussing the responsibilities of peoples, a convenient topic for international polemics. We fail to ask ourselves a preliminary and capital question: Can the notion of responsibility be applied to a people? Philosophers, moralists, and jurists generally admit that responsibility is based on human freedom, the reality of which, moreover, is denied by some. This freedom, however, if it does exist, can only be individual. How then could responsibility be different? Even if one admits that a man can be free, how can a group of human beings be free? It has no will; at the most it has impulses, tendencies, more or less habitual types of behavior. Shall we say that the group can make majority decisions? In that case, the minority could not be held responsible. In a parliament, in any body in which decisions are made in that way, the members of the minority never fail to say that they are not responsible, when it becomes clear that a law or a measure which has been accepted by vote is unpopular or harmful.

Who is responsible for wars?

Peoples are never consulted in the major decisions which, such as the decision to go to war, set them against one another. It is difficult for them to be consulted; such decisions must be made quickly and elements known only to a small number of persons must be taken into account. Decisions are thus reserved for the small group. Whether the government involved is an absolute monarchy, a dictatorship, or a democratic republic, there is not much difference in the way the decision is reached.[102]

In such cases, governments often feel themselves bound by alliances which restrict their freedom of choice. Aren't they really free to apply such alliances or to disregard them? In 1939, the French government declared war on Germany under its allliance with Poland. In 1938, it had neglected its alliance with Czechoslovakia, allowing that country to be crushed by Hitler. It must be added that alliances are always concluded without consulting the people. The French people were no more consulted about concluding the Polish or the Czechoslovakian alliance than they had been earlier about the alliance with Russia. That is an abuse common to all regimes. In this case, the democracies adhered to the custom of the absolute monarchy, a custom logical in that kind of government, but which becomes truly scandalous in regimes which claim to be founded on the will of the people.

In absolute monarchies alliances were the sovereign's business, as was war; the army was his army, and the people were hardly involved in a war, which was conducted by small numbers of mercenaries. It affected the people only if it was of long duration and became expensive, or if the country was invaded. Responsibility then would fall back on the monarch; even a king like Louis XIV, whose prestige was enormous, became unpopular near the end of his reign because his wars had turned out badly.

Today war involves the whole population; all men are called up, expenditures are enormous compared to what they used to be, damage is infinitely greater, and the civilian population is just as threatened by danger as the combattants themselves; in future wars, they may well be more threatened. It would therefore seem natural and right that people should not be thrown into war against their will, without anyone's having taken the trouble to ascertain their opinion in the matter. Although it is not possible to take opinion polls when war is imminent, alliances, often the causes of conflict, are concluded in peacetime, when there is ample time for discussing the pros and cons, and for studying conditions, advantages, and risks.

Before binding the French people to Poland, wouldn't it have been correct to inform them that this alliance would make them run the risk of a war over the Danzig Corridor? (Foch *dixit*)? It is possible, but not certain, that the prospect of fighting for a cause so foreign to their interests would have appealed to the French. If they had accepted it, French diplomacy would have been made stronger. We could have said, "French people require that this boundary between Germany and Poland be preserved." The Germans, who were reluctant to believe this, would have been put on notice. Since there was no such vote, and since they saw France abandon Czechoslovakia, they could only be skeptical about her will to fight for the corridor. Whether the alliance was approved or rejected by the people, in either case the chances for war would have been reduced.

If governments up to now have not found it good to consult the people on a declaration of war or on an alliance, might this not be because they have found a way to avoid the responsibilities? It is a very simple way—one puts them off onto the opponent. With a well organized propaganda campaign, with the help of nationalism, nothing is easier than to persuade a people that the aggressor is the other fellow. We must recognize moreover that with modern weapons there are and there will be an increasing number of doubtful cases. The "determining of the aggressor," a problem which had caused the late League of Nations to grow pale with study, is one of these riddles on which no one is near to reaching agreement. Although there are sufficiently clear cases, such as the Korean War of 1950 and the aggressions of Hitler against Poland, there are others over which uncertainty or a suspicion of a general responsibility hovers.

One sees that when we go back into the past, the responsibilities seem easier to determine than they are today. For the war of 1870 there is no problem—the responsibilities are shared by Prussia and France, by Bismarck and Napoleon III. For the war of 1914, the question is definitely more complicated. If we consider the alliances and the policy of the great powers, the atmosphere in which the conflict broke out and its premonitory symptoms, the diplomatic and military measures which preceded it, it seems difficult to draw any definite conclusions from them. Neither are the intentions always perfectly clear, nor is the effect indisputable of a given step which was taken (or of one which wasn't but might have been). One sometimes has the impression that most of the heads of state and of governments did not want war, but let themselves be drawn into it by blunders, weakness, or negligence. Others talk of a machine which, once it had been started, could not be stopped. Anyone can assign the responsibilities as he sees fit. The only thing which seems incontestable is that each nation has its share of them.

In 1939, the crushing responsibility of Hitler stands above all the rest, but it does not eliminate them; the U.S.S.R.'s responsibility is considerable, since a few days before the war, it concluded the agreement with Germany for the division of Poland. That of France and of England is no small matter either; they rushed into the conflict at a time when they were incapable of mounting the offensive indispensable for saving their ally, and when, consequently, nothing obliged them to enter. Their responsibility is even greater in the preceding period, at the time of Munich, and particularly in 1936, when Hitler could easily have been eliminated. We could incriminate the whole Franco–British policy of the period between

France and Germany

the two wars. After a victory like that of 1918, victors who cannot prevent a new war twenty years later are inept.

It is a matter, of course, of government leaders and perhaps also of opinion, and of those who are supposed to create it and who, instead of criticizing and rectifying the policy of their governments, generally encourage it. It seems difficult, in the present world situation, to talk of the responsibilities of peoples in war.

Peoples who used to be bellicose

However, when we observe certain constants in a people's policy, can't we attribute to that people a character which would determine their policy? The Roman people showed itself for centuries to be fairly aggressive; can't we say therefore that it was bellicose? Let us remember that acting in a certain way because of character is the opposite of what we commonly call responsibility; character stems from fatality, not from freedom of choice. Popular judgment, however, is not so particular about it. If another people seems to be acting in a way which it considers blameworthy (i.e., annoying to it), it will criticize it all the more because its character so determined things. There are some who hold the ancient Romans in horror, since they see them as harsh, brutal, and pitiless. Wasn't this in their nature? Well, too bad for their nature, for that is precisely what is being condemned. This way of seeing things is understandable; since the life of peoples is longer than that of individuals, we understand that the one who has an aggressive and powerful neighbor, who has suffered at his hand from many attacks, invasions, and terri-

194

torial amputations, makes his neighbor responsible, without analyzing the concept of responsibility. If it were true, as some people think, that Germany constantly attacked France over a period of fifteen hundred years (or putting it the other way around, if France constantly attacked Germany), could we not say that one country is responsible for the misfortunes of the other?

The answer to the question would be of an historical nature; we shall not dwell on it here, since we have already reviewed rapidly the relations of the two peoples. It follows from this that although the Germans invaded France a certain number of times, the French did the same thing to Germany. It would be childish to try to add up these invasions. According to the ups and downs of politics, when one of the nations found itself stronger and was not occupied somewhere else, it could turn against the other. France has carried out more conquests against Germany than Germany against France; from the annexation of the Three Bishoprics in the sixteenth century, to those of Alsace in the seventeenth, of Lorraine in the eighteenth, France constantly encroached upon her neighbor (to say nothing of the left bank of the Rhine during the Revolution, but which was held only briefly). The only German conquest was that of Alsace–Lorraine in 1870.

It might be added (1) that France, in the course of centuries, fought with all her neighbors, with some, like England, more often and for longer periods than with Germany; (2) that Germany also waged war along all her borders; (3) that the two peoples always had the reputation of being fighters and warmongers. (The Teutons and the Gauls were considered so by the Romans. But could the French, heirs of the Gauls, Romans, and Germans, be peaceful?) (4) that the character of a people may change. The Romans, who had conquered the world, fell when attacked by the barbarians; had they ceased to be fighters? The French have hardly been fighters since the time of Napoleon. It is doubtful that the Germans are still. And what of the Italians, the heirs of the Romans?

All young, dynamic peoples go through periods of aggressiveness. The Romans, at first an insignificant tribe, conquered the whole Mediterranean basin. The Celts overran Europe from Great Britain to Asia Minor. The Mongols advanced from the farthest reaches of Asia as far as Central Europe, and the Russians followed the same path in the opposite direction, from the Vistula to the Pacific. The Arabs, leaving the Red Sea area, occupied Spain and drove all the way to Poitiers. The English, Dutch, Spanish, Portuguese, and French swarmed over all the continents. Since ancient times, all peoples of a certain vitality have overflowed the confines of their habitat, and without asking permission of those whom they invaded.

What distinguishes the German from the others is the fact that he has acted with less skill, or that he has been less well served by luck. While the Russians and the Arabs were still deploying over vast territories, the Germans saw their territory shrinking, from the Middle Ages on, and increasingly in modern times.[103] Was it the fault of their leaders, or was it fate? Both, no doubt. France also tried, with Napoleon, to attain dimensions unrelated to her real strength. She failed, and nothing is farther from her mind than starting over again. The situation of Europe and the world no longer permits either people such undertakings.

The question of Alsace and the Franco–German conflict

A careful examination of history shows that the Franco–German conflict goes back in reality to 1870, or at the very most, to 1813, when the German people united against Napoleon. This conflict raises a question of responsibility on which it is difficult to reach any agreement. Although Alsace was not the major cause of the war in which France lost it—the cause was rather German unity—it long constituted a dispute which, added to other disputes, could be the last straw. When Alsace was annexed by Germany, it became the symbol of a hostility which did not soften with time. The French blamed the Germans for having taken a French province from them. The Germans replied that it was German. "You took it from us; we have merely recovered our own property."

On matters of annexation, the German and French points of view differ. The Germans think that any country or province which is German by race and speech rightfully belongs to them. Accordingly, France is the major responsible party for the quarrel over Alsace, since she annexed it three centuries ago when it was German. The French retort that what the Alsatians were and what they thought in 1648 no longer count; the only thing that matters is their present desire to be French, a desire which they showed during the Revolution. They demonstrated it unanimously in 1871 and again in 1918. They are therefore part of the French nation.

The French add that the rule which the Germans cite as their authority, that a territory belongs to a given state by virtue of the language of its inhabitants, was not valid in the century of Richelieu and Louis XIV. In those days a sovereign annexed a province when he could, without concerning himself about those living in it. Belgium, which had belonged to the Holy Empire, had passed to the Duke of Burgundy, then to the Hapsburgs of Austria, then to the Hapsburgs of Spain, only to come back again to the Austrians under the Treaty of Utrecht. Divided into French departments during the Revolution and the empire, it was incorporated into Holland in 1815, and finally won independence in 1830. This is only an example chosen at random; many others could be found in Germany's history.

It is pointless to prolong the discussion, since the "principle of nationalities" invoked by Germany and by France is not understood by them in the same way. The Germans are convinced that the French have wronged them by Gallicizing the Alsatians, just as the French are convinced that they have acted with justice in giving them a fatherland of their choice. For the Germans, nationality is based on race and language, for the French on the right of peoples to self-determination.

This discussion did not remain academic. Fed on sentimental elements, maintained by the self-respect of the two adversaries, it would dictate their policies for almost a century. It ended only when the German people, after the return of Alsace to France in 1918 and 1945 bowed before the *fait accompli*.[104] But this case offers a curious example of the way in which certain conflicts, really started by some sovereign's action, are little by little transferred to the peoples involved and finally belong as much to public opinion as to the will of government leaders. A province which at first hardly interested the French (it didn't speak their language) was annexed to the kingdom by the king's will, or rather by his minister's will, Louis XIV then being ten years old. Mazarin was no doubt acting in accord with political and strategic planning.[105] Perhaps he did not think that this conquest of Alsace was irrevocable; in a negotiation, for example, it might be used as exchange—ransom for a defeat, or exchange for lost provinces which had been French for a longer period.[106] The conquest was, however, little by little incorporated into the national patrimony; it is difficult to believe that those responsible for it could foresee this development or could guess that Alsace would weigh so heavily on the relations of two great nations. In becoming integrated with popular sentiment, through its appeal to the passions of both peoples, to their sentiment of justice and national solidarity, it would finally make them responsible themselves for a conflict which was originally the affair of the ruler and as such, more easily resolved. As experience has shown, there is hardly any longer a solution, except by war, for a quarrel which affects the feeling of the masses. To avoid war over Alsace, the leaders of the two countries would have had to take the quarrel into their own hands, removing it from the passions of the crowds. It is not certain that they had the requisite authority; William II, an authoritarian ruler in appearance, was hardly less obedient to the rip tides of public opinion than were the ministers of the Third Republic.

France and Germany

As a problem of responsibility, the Alsatian question remains without solution for France and Germany. Their points of view will never coincide, and it would be impossible to fix responsibility to everyone's satisfaction. The problem will disappear only as time makes men forget and grow indifferent to it.

Are the German people responsible for Hitler?

Germany's policy since Bismarck is sometimes attributed to German nationalism, to national socialism, to what is called imperialism, German militarism, or simply "Germanism." We must be careful about making so many "isms," which express only abstractions, responsible for human actions. We have tried above to show that it is difficult to define precisely what "militarism or "nationalism" are. It is men who act, not ideas or words; although ideas and words have a certain active force, no one can measure it, since in every man there are other ideas, feelings, and interests acting at the same time.

To choose an example, is Germany's entrance into war in 1914 and her defeat to be explained by William II's nationalism or militarism? The Kaiser was not only a German nationalist, as was proper, but also a monarch imbued with Prussian traditions, a man afflicted with certain complexes in respect to the king of England, his uncle.[107] By virtue of monarchical solidarity and the memories of the Holy Empire of which he was co-heir with the Hapsburgs, he wanted to be faithful to Francis Joseph. These and other sentiments all influenced his decisions. And yet it was not his feelings, but his diplomatic errors, which had the greatest influence on

200

Germany's fate, since she could have had Russia and England as friends instead of enemies.

A responsibility which has been much discussed since 1945 is that of the German people in the behavior of Hitler. For some, Hitler is identified with Germany, while others reject purely and simply the notion of popular responsibility, on the grounds that in a totalitarian regime the chief is solely responsible, the people having no means to act by itself or to exercise any influence whatsoever. To express an opinion different from the dictator's is enough to sentence one to the gallows or the deportation camp. Elections and plebiscites, controlled and rigged, always give him ninety-nine or even one hundred per cent of the votes. He hides from the people everything it must not know, and those who do find out are careful to keep their mouths shut, as there are spies and informers everywhere.

Contrary to what has often been thought, particularly outside Germany, the German people never called Hitler to power. At the last free elections, on November 6, 1932, he obtained thrity-two per cent of the votes. A party leader with a third of the population behind him does not automatically become head of the government. It was the president of the Reich, Hindenburg, who appointed Hitler chancellor on January 30, 1933, and he acted without being forced and without anyone's expecting it. National socialism was in fact losing momentum, four per cent of its voters having abandoned it in the three months which followed the elections of July 31, 1932.

This question arises nevertheless—how can a man with only a third of the people supporting him gain unlimited support for himself in a few months, suppress all the rights of seventy million people, without anyone's protesting or looking up? Doesn't that require an almost general complicity, a strange passivity, the total abdication of those in positions of control, who could have done something, could have brought others to fall in behind them? Isn't it strange that neither in the Prussian police, considered to be republican, nor in the army, which was not republican but not national socialist either, nor among the workers, who might have staged a general strike, no one brandished the standard of a revolt which might have brought millions of men to their feet?

The answer one gets is that Hitler's police was quickly and strongly organized, thanks to the S.A. and the S.S., that the police of the Weimar Republic had already been emasculated by von Papen's government, that the army followed the Führer, that it was difficult for the workers to demonstrate, with six million unemployed; that the last election had given six million votes to the communists (who were not identical with the six million unemployed, but who had always adopted the policy of the worst political elements, and who played Hitler's game until the day he eliminated them). That may all be true, but it doesn't satisfy our desire to know. When Napoleon had himself crowned emperor, he had great deeds behind him; Hitler's record was merely thousands of mass meetings, where he had always repeated the same old slogans. Moreover, the Napoleonic regime was a paradise of gentleness compared to national socialism. This is perhaps one of those cases to which we might apply the old adage, "Every people has the government it deserves." For after all, counting the votes cast and noting that the majority is opposed is not enough to measure the responsibility of a people. Isn't the origin of the catastrophe to be sought in the spirit which moved the people, in the acts or failures to act of those who could act, in the abstentions of millions who had at least a ballot with which to influence destiny, and failed to use it?

One of the best contemporary German philosophers, Karl Jaspers, has sought to distinguish political responsibility from moral responsibility.[108] "We bear," he says, "the 'political' responsibility for the regime which was ours, for its acts, for the starting of war in a world historical situation like that one, and for the character of the leader whom we permitted to lead us." The partnership which binds together all the members of one people and binds it to its government obliges it to bear the consequences of its acts, however painful they may be. This does not mean, Jaspers goes on to say, that the German people have a moral responsibility. Only a small minority deserves punishment for crimes it committed. Since responsibility is strictly an individual matter, a whole people could not bear it in the moral and penal sense of the word. It is each man's duty to "settle his accounts with himself, to ask himself before his conscience to what extent he is responsible for the tragic events which have afflicted his country and all humanity along with it."

Aren't these distinctions, which appear reasonable in principle, a bit too subtle for the common mortal? They have the defect of separating the moral from the political, which many cannot permit. Jaspers recognizes this. "The behavior which engaged our responsibility," he says, "is based on general political conditions which also have a moral character, since they help determine the ethics of individuals . . . There is no absolute cleavage between politics and the human condition . . . Political liberty bears within it a moral element."[109]

It is normal that on such a difficult and complex question opinions should vary. However, whatever share that one can or is willing to give to circumstances (Hindenburg's responsibility, Hitler as an unusual personage, unpredictable actions, etc.), the German people will do well to accept its share of guilt—and that is in its own interest. Would not refusing it be a confession of ignorance, passivity, and callousness? Wouldn't this be, above all, compromising Germany's future, declaring oneself ready to undertake new ventures, revolts, or revolutions? If the Germans had no responsibility in the Hitlerian drama, that would mean that they are disclaiming competence before any similar accident which might again befall them; that they would be disposed to accept it with all its consequences; and, in a word, that would mean that policy of their country does not interest them, does not even concern them, that they would hand it over to the first charlatan who might come along who would be willing to take it, and who could persuade them to follow him. In other words, they would hand their country's policy over to chance.

War criminals

One point which deserves particular mention is responsibility in the conducting of war. In a totalitarian regime the chief is theoretically the only responsible party. Hitler always accepted his responsibilities; he does not appear to have tried to push them off onto others, but practically, he could not see and know everything. His subordinates, both big and little, each had his field of action in which he was almost independent. It was not Hitler who gave the order to destroy Oradour; he did give the order to destroy Paris, but it was not obeyed. On the other hand, it can be admitted that he is responsibile for the death of millions of Jews; Himmler could not take such a grave decision independently.

The last war was much more cruel than those of other times. Millions of civilians, women and children, died in Russia and in Poland through the fault of the Germans, and not only through the fault of their leaders. Ten thousand Polish officers were massacred at Katyn by the Russians, who also raped thousands (some say millions) of women. Four million Germans perished in bombings or flight.

On the German side, national socialism has a big share of the responsibility. Its doctrine dictated not only a pitiless war, but also the massacre or displacement of whole populations to make room for the conquerors. The callousness which it had cultivated in peacetime in large segments of the population (Hitler Youth, S.A., S.S., Gestapo) was only heightened by the effect of war. By its nature, national socialism attracted individuals from the lowest levels of society, potential or real convicts, who behaved according to their instincts. It is responsible for the acts which horrified the world, because it placed in positions of command the vilest and most cruel men, and spread this cruelty through its propaganda and its examples.

If several thousand butchers cannot deny their responsibility, the mass of those who were called later the "little Nazis" (there were about eleven million of them) was composed essentially of followers, men who had joined the party to do as everyone else was doing, to improve their situation, or in order not to lose it. It was a superficial, imprudent action of postwar allied policy to try to turn these eleven million into culprits, to require them to furnish proof of innocence. Are we to be surprised that this comedy of justice, soon turned over to the Germans themselves, has resulted in an almost general acquittal, therefore in a fiasco? You don't cut eleven million men away from a people's life unless you suppress them. These "little Nazis" eluded the interrogations on the horrors they had not committed, perhaps which they had not known about. It would have been courageous of them to have spoken out publicly against these horrors, but civic courage is not common, in Germany or anywhere else.

The Nüremberg Tribunal was an attempt to bring the big war criminals to justice; it was laudable in its intent, but also vain and dangerous. Although it is true that the tribunal included eminent judges, that their efforts were conscientious, that most of those sentenced appear to have been guilty,[110] the very existence of such a tribunal raised objections. Can one set oneself up as the judge of one's enemies, that is, as judge and plaintiff, without running the risk of being suspected of partiality? Certain of these judges, the Russians for example, were suspected of the same crimes as the Germans. Only a tribunal composed of neutrals would have had the necessary qualifications, and the neutrals would have de-

clined the honor. German judges would have been preferable
if it was desired that the verdict should be accepted by the
German people, and that was essential.

Did the powers involved foresee the inevitable consequences of their justice? In making themselves judges of the
conquered enemy, the conquerors created a precedent which
will be followed in the next war, and the victor, whoever he
is, will be seen condemning the loser, even if he is innocent,
as a "war criminal." As Field Marshal Montgomery has said,
"Since the Nüremberg trial, it has become a crime to make
war without winning it."[111]

[102]President Wilson took it upon himself in 1917 to de
clare war on Germany, and in 1939, M. Daladier did the same.
The latter was reproached for not having consulted parliament, but what parliament ever refused to support the
government which had declared war or wanted to?

[103]Cf. the earlier chapter, "A Conqueror without Conquests."

[104]We should perhaps use a question mark in saying
"bowed." We note, however, that during the Weimar Republic and the reign of Hitler, although there may have been
some German intriguing in Alsace, the German press made
scarcely any mention of the province.

[105]According to certain historians, the annexation of Alsace was not in the plans of Richelieu, whose work was continued by Mazarin.

[106]In 1712, when peace negotiations began at Utrecht,
France was at first in a bad posture. The emperor claimed
Alsace along with Strasbourg and the three bishoprics. The
French victory at Denain caused him to relinquish his claims.
It is understandable that if the military situation had forced
him to it, the king of France would more easily have given
up a province recently conquered from Germany than old
French provinces.

[107]Although Edward VII had died in 1910, the feelings he had inspired in William II during his lifetime persisted.

[108]Cf. Karl Jaspers, *Die Schuldfrage,* translated into French under the title: *La Culpabilité allemande [German Guilt].*

[109]Jaspers distinguishes a third kind of culpability, "metaphysical" culpability, which seems rather to be reserved to professional philosophers, or at least to those of a philosophical turn of mind.

[110]Reservations may be made concerning some of those found guilty, such as Baron von Neurath, accused of "genocide" for having prepared the transfer of a number of Czechoslovakians. Whether or not these transfers were ever carried out or not has never been said, but in 1945, three million Sudeten Germans were driven out and their property was confiscated, without President Béneš and the Czechoslovakian government, who were responsible, having been accused of genocide. See on this subject the statement of the American newspaperman, R. W. Cooper, in *The Nuremberg Trial.* He could not be considered suspect, since he is anti-German.

[111]Compare this remark with that by General MacArthur, the American commander-in-chief in Japan: "When General Tojo was found guilty, I thought that I'd do well never to lose a war." Are we to think that sometimes military men may understand justice better than professional judges do?

CHAPTER 18

Democracy in France and in Germany

THE problem of the responsibility of the German people in the Hitlerian adventure is closely linked to that of democracy in Germany. The very definition of a "democracy" is that it is a people which assumes responsibility for its policy. If the people abdicates and falls into the hands of one man or a small group, it is refusing the responsibility of conducting its own affairs. Such was formerly the custom when kings and their companions could pass as the protectors of the people, but times have changed. A people which evades the task of self-government exposes itself to regimes much worse than absolute monarchy, which, in certain periods, was tolerable or even necessary. The political evolution of Germany is different from that of the large western nations; liberty there did not go through a slow development as it did in England.

And unlike France, Germany had no violent upheaval to overthrow the old order with one stroke. Its developmental line is broken, and democracy is both old and new there. In the Middle Ages, many free towns, "towns of the empire," governed themselves under the remote patronage of the emperor—there were the Hanseatic ports like Hamburg, the cities of the southwest like Frankfort, Augsburg, and Nüremberg. The southwest is a close relative of Switzerland, which also belonged to the empire and separated from it in the thirteenth century.[112]

However, the prolonged division of this Germany, maintaining as it did the trusteeship of the princes in a multitude of little states, the particular character of Prussia, and finally the Reformation, were to mark Germany's political development strongly. It has been said that the true German revolution was Luther's Reformation, that it consumed the strength of the German people, engendering an internal war which culminated more than a century later in the frightful Thirty Years' War. Protestantism gave a strong shock to men's minds, and provoked the Counter Reformation. It inspired in most Germans in respect to religion an attitude which was quite different from that of the French philosophers of the eighteenth century. Catholics and Protestants finally tolerated each other in Germany; but Lutheranism, recognizing religion as the province of the ruler, was not democratic like the non-conformist churches of England and the United States; it went to the aid of authority.

After 1815, the evolution of the German people would not have been very different from that of the French if its obsession with unity had not turned it towards Prussia. There were many liberals in Germany; the Frankfort Assembly of 1848 had a liberal majority, but liberalism was hidden by the Prussian strength which alone appeared capable of unifying Germany.[118]

The regime of Prussia, later Germany, under William I and William II was not an authoritarian regime, but that of a semi-democratic monarchy. There was rather a good deal of freedom in it, if not complete freedom. Although the government was not answerable to the Reichstag, that body was not at all powerless. Remarkable men sat in it, and Bismarck himself, in the serious matter of the Kulturkampf had to capitulate to the Catholics under Windthorst. The Kaiser was often criticized or caricaturized, and the socialists—"my socialists," as he referred to them—increased from 351 thousand in 1874 to more than four million in 1912. What was lacking for the creation of a democratic atmosphere was a true liberal party; Prussian predominance had made the liberal element deviate, and it became "national liberal," that is, tainted with nationalism. The influence of military men, and of the Junkers, that last vestige of feudalism, persisted until 1918.

The Weimar Republic came very close to being able to establish democracy in Germany. Despite the difficulties that it encountered because of the action of nationalists, national socialists, and communists, the new regime might have lived, if it had been able to create an army devoted to it, and to prohibit the formation of para-military organizations which stirred up the German people with their massive manifestations and later broke the people's will to resist when Hitler approached power. Since the army was neutral, the country found that it had been handed over to the S.A. and the S.S.

A new regime which clashes with strong opposition must have strength. The Weimar Republic succumbed because it was not able, or was unwilling, to provide itself with force, and not because it applied the democratic system more or less rigorously. It adopted the proportional system which led, people said, to the breaking up of parties, but it did not prevent Hitler's party from eclipsing all the others. Energy and the combative spirit were lacking in the leaders. They believed that democracy required mildness, good nature, and fair play in the face of brutal, unscrupulous opponents. The majority of the nation, which voted up to 1932 for the republic, was no less democratic than people in other countries, but the non-committed and the malcontents let themselves be charmed by Hitler's mad appeals; they found in him the inspiring leader democracy had been unable to supply.

Any regime, whatever its principles and its rules of conduct, must adapt its conduct to that of its adversaries; if they are brutal and ambitious, it can be dangerous to handle them gently. Since the democracy which has been in power in recent years in Germany has not known any adversaries worthy of the name, we do not know if it would better able the democracy of Weimar to stand against them. It has drawn certain lessons from the latter's example, and its smooth functioning has, up to now, surprised the world. Nowhere has the head of a democratic government remained so long in power as Chancellor Adenauer, no one has had the same authority, no one has pursued as successfully the re-establishing of his country. Certain of his ideas may be criticized, but the difficult situation of Germany from the exterior point of view is due to the four occupying powers, who at the end of the war could not give her unity, although they said they desired it. To get it back, it is possible that the Chancellor's successors may someday have to follow another policy. As that policy has not yet been formulated, Adenauer cannot be blamed for holding to his own.

Despite this unexpected success, one wonders sometimes if perhaps exceptional circumstances have not operated in Germany, if the German is truly a democrat and if democracy is solidly seated there.

At first glance, the average German is probably not so fundamentally democratic, even today, when appearances are favorable, as the Swiss or American citizen. Democracy in Switzerland is several hundred years old. In the United States it is younger, but is re-enforced with a theory which has become a veritable dogma. There is certainly nothing similar in Germany. The dominating tradition there is that of the strong, if not authoritarian state. The tradition comes from Prussia, and the socialists do not denounce it; it seems to fit in with the ideal of the social-democrats.

As this tradition is found both on the right and the left, among conservatives and socialists alike, one wonders if the evolution toward a practical monopoly of two big political parties which is appearing might not lead to a more or less authoritarian regime. In Germany, liberalism lost its moment a century ago; will it now be able to prosper there, when it is declining almost everywhere else?

France and Germany

Of the two qualities, opposite and complimentary, which democracy requires, the taste for freedom and for discipline, the French have the first, the Germans the second, and the Anglo–Saxons have both. No one knows if the incomplete democrats will one day join the one hundred per cent democrats. Lacking one or the other of these qualities, what people would be sure of evolving in an orderly and normal way?

It has been said that the Germans are unpredictable, changeable, and not very reliable, quick to turn about brusquely. And what of the French? Who could have foreseen before 1789 the Revolution, the Terror, Napoleon, the two Restorations, the new revolutions of 1830 and 1848, followed by the Second Empire, the Third Republic, the Commune, the so-called National Revolution of 1940, the Fourth Republic, and finally, the Fifth? As far as political upheaval goes, the French record beats the German by far. We must not complain about the speck in our neighbor's eye in order to neglect the beam in ours. In Germany, optimists can hope that the great evolutionary (not revolutionary) tradition which has always ruled Germanic peoples such as the British, Dutch, and Scandinavians, will finally be imposed there too.[114]

The Germans and the French had a weakness for political ideologies, although they didn't favor the same ones. Do they still have this? On one side, the predilection was for constructions of pure reason, while the others preferred systems described as scientific, such as Marx's materialism, or biological racism. The German doctrines expressed a will to power incompatible with a sobered Europe. France's doc-

214

trines, after having restored to the individual his "natural rights," pushed him on to a continuous and exaggerated claim, to the scorn of the authority requisite in any community. Outside of France, they developed an explosive nationalism which, under the guise of the right of peoples, risked destroying boundaries and destroying the work of integration accomplished by modern states.[115]

Is the world guided by the ideologies of the Revolution or by the two poles marked by the two German systems? A difficult question. It seems that the German theories as well as the French have flown from the small Franco–German area of the world to stir up other continents. The idea of the self-determination of peoples has roused France's former colonies against her. Asia is both communists and racist. Have the systems which were born in France and Germany ceased to serve them, and will these two nations now have to solve their problems according to more practical and realistic rules?

The evolution of France over the past fifteen years gives us democrats cause for reflection. If the sovereignty of the people must be general indifference, if freedom must be the shameless pursuit of individual interests, if parties must be coteries which are blind to the public interest, if power must be a ball for them to play with, what is then left of a regime which Western men, out of old habit, believe to be irreplaceable? A great American democrat, Walter Lippmann, denounced its weaknesses long before our last crisis. Observing that democratic states had not been able to establish a real peace after the two world wars they had won, he wrote, "The people has won a power which it is incapable of exercising

. . . Let us say that it must have the possibility of giving or of refusing its consent to those who govern it, to what is asked of it, to what is proposed to it, to what the government has already accomplished. The people can elect governors, it can appoint them, it can approve or disapprove their action, but it cannot govern . . . A weakening of the capacity to govern which borders on paralysis is the cause of the headlong decline, the catastrophic decline of Western society, which can involve the fall of the West, if we don't stop it, if we don't turn back."[116]

The question goes beyond Germany and France. Democratic nations think they have found a definitive formula, which they offer against communism and fascism. This formula shows everywhere traces of age and of lack of adaptation to modern life. It is not enough to offer the social or socialist tendency, and the liberal tendency, sometimes in regular balancing as with the Anglo–Saxons, sometimes in the anarchical cohort of multiple parties as in France. Any people which wishes to survive in today's harsh competition will need a stable government, with men of experience and technicians rather than talkers. It will require of all members of the community a less negligent and a more efficient collaboration. The people, if it cannot govern itself, will have to follow attentively the policies of those who do govern and learn to judge them. It will be particularly necessary to overcome the apathy of the masses, who do not even have a minimum of training for citizenship (the middle class no more than the working class), who are interested only in cars, television, movie stars, and "perfect crimes," who hand over their fate to the politicians, except when they make a demand on the welfare state.

The German democrats are not very different from the French or any others, with this shade of difference, however, that after terrible experiences, they trust a little more a regime which is new to them. But weren't the regimes which have risen in the last half-century born of the errors and omissions which are part of this one? If it wants to fight successfully, it will have to revise its organization and its methods.

Only then will we be able to judge it, in France as in Germany; in Germany, democracy is taking its first steps, in France it is showing great deterioration. Of the two peoples, the better democrat will be the one most capable of finding new ways.

[112]Cf. Machiavelli, *Report on the Things of Germany:* "Germany's power resides certainly much more in her communes than in her princes . . . The free communes of the empire are the very sinew of Germany."

[113]We have cited above (pp. 48–49) Quinet's prophetic lines, written forty years before the event. "It is surprising," he goes on, "that the only popular government beyond the Rhine is almost the only one which has the form of a despotism . . . It is an intelligent, active, ambitious despotism, needing nothing more than a man."

Had Quinet foreseen Bismarck?

[114]Cf. Winston Churchill, *A History of the English Speaking Peoples, I: The Birth of Britain:* "There is scarcely any doubt that there were found in the conception of tribal life of the Germanic nation many principles which enjoy the admiration of our contemporaries."

[115]Cf. Albert Sorel, *La Patriotisme allemand sort des droits de l'homme.*

[116]From *Twilight of the Democracies?* (1950).

CHAPTER 19

Reversal of Alliances

ARE we to say that Germany's international position since the last war has been determined by her domestic policy? Or is it the other way around? The division of her territory between the Western powers and the U.S.S.R. naturally implied a democratic regime in the west and a Soviet regime in the east. The two Germanys could not escape the influences of the occupying powers, especially East Germany, where it was not only a question of influences, but of restrictions. In the west, a democracy closely linked to America, England, and France was established. Was this regime, while keeping its distance with the east, really required to burn its bridges with the other Germany? The suggestions of the occupying powers were not always orders. Relations might have been established with the Democratic (People's) Republic, the three Western powers could have been pushed to negotiate with Moscow, and the key position of Germany even used to exert a certain pressure—to put it frankly, a certain blackmail—on the protecting governments, so as to reach the essential goal of all Germans, the reunification of their country.

It didn't turn out that way. The German government was always irreproachably loyal to the Occidentals, especially the Americans who were running the show. Between Bonn and Washington there was never the shadow of a cloud; was this because the Germans, having no army and receiving material aid from the United States, believed they were required to make their policy agree with American policy? Or because their political tendencies were the same? In fact, the Federal Republic, having many fewer communists than France or Italy, and not having had since its founding any socialist governments as France, England, Belgium, Holland, and the Scandinavian countries had had, was, like the United States, a liberal-conservative state.

It might be said that Germany would have adopted another policy, if she had had, as Austria did, a central government. The Vienna government, Christian and socialist at the same time, did not hesitate to declare itself neutral in order to obtain the end of Allied occupation. A central German government could have and ought to have done likewise; but it would have been difficult for it, with one part of Germany being occupied by the Western powers, the other by the U.S.S.R., to conclude any alliance with either. Since the occupying powers had had the unfortunate idea of eliminating a central government, didn't the political division of Germany

France and Germany

become inevitable thereby?[117] The division, perhaps, but it is not certain that the total isolation of the two parts was inevitable. France, England, the United States itself, have relations with Soviet Russia—why not anti-Soviet Germany with Soviet or Sovietized Germany? Certainly the west had great attractions for East Germany, and there was the possibility of alliance—but isn't the aspiration to unity greater than all alliances?

Whatever the reasons which motivated the Germans to ally themselves with the west, we can only note that they have done it, and that consequently everything has happened as if her ideological position took primacy in her eyes over national imperatives. Opting without reticence for Western democracy, she associated herself at the same time with its foreign policy and joined the anti-Soviet bloc.

There resulted from this a reversal of the alliances of the last war, not so much for Germany as for her new allies (she had fought against both Soviet Russia and the Western powers). She retained one of her adversaries as an enemy and allied herself to the other.

History teaches us that reversals of alliances are often in the interest of those who decide to make them. A nation's policy is a continual adaptation to circumstances over which one does not always have control These circumstances can require a change in policy, a change to which one generally brings oneself too late. When France, in 1756, allied herself to Austria, that power had long since ceased to represent a threat to her. If Louis XIV, who had understood this, had concluded that alliance, he would have avoided serious difficulties for himself and his successor. It took the rise of a threatening Prussia to make Paris draw closer to Vienna. Yet most of the French did not think Prussia was a threat, and went on tossing bouquets to the king of Prussia.

The same is true of the Entente Cordiale, which began with Louis Philippe. The word dates from that time, but the thing itself was achieved only in 1904, and had it been achieved earlier, the war of 1870 would not have taken place. We can go back still further: on the eve of the Revolution, after two Franco–British wars, Mirabeau and Talleyrand, the best political minds of the day, already were demanding an alliance with England, which could have prevented the wars of the Revolution and the empire.[118]

The alliance, or at least the entente with Germany became automatically necessary after the First World War. If it had been achieved, would the second war have been possible? Although the situation of Europe and the world was not what it is today, Germany and France could have come to an understanding.

After the Second World War, experience could show that this entente was relatively easy, despite the difference in the situation and in the dispositions of the two peoples. It was no longer a question of possibility, but one of necessity.

It was not France which took the initiative of dividing Germany into two zones instead of four, nor of forming an anti-Soviet bloc and bringing Germany into it. France followed because she could not do otherwise. Her geographic position, her various economic, political, and military interests, placed her in the Western camp. The European movement which was beginning to take shape at the time, might bring her closer to Germany, but its aim was not military. At bottom it was *chance* and the force of events which brought it about that Germany and France found themselves side by side, on the same side of the barricade, without having sought or desired it.

Before examining this situation and the perspectives it opens up it seems difficult to avoid this question: Was it inevitable? At Potsdam on August 2, 1945, a preliminary treaty on Germany had been signed by Great Britain, the United States, and the U.S.S.R., which France would join. Why was this accord, which normally would have been confirmed and defined a little later, never applied? Is it fitting to mention Versailles, where the impotency of the Western Allies had already been made manifest? Whatever criticisms we make of this Potsdam agreement, it did define a *modus vivendi* between Germany and her conquerors. A European status could come of it, a viable status, but Europe would be divided into two camps, whose opposition would continue to grow more serious, and Germany would find herself cut in two, contrary to the arrangements undertaken in respect to her.

The current response is that this opposition was fated, that between communists and anti-communists no entente was possible. Moscow having tried some years later to seize Greece and Korea, and having already seized Czechoslovakia, we can entertain no illusions about Soviet aims. Yet other countries occupied by the four conquerors—Austria, for example—have not experienced the same cutting up as Germany. Could it not have been avoided for her, since the agreement of the four[119] provided for *German* economic ministries for all Germany? They could have been enough to assure a certain provisional structure, which would have been completed later with a political structure.

Why were these ministries never created? Was it ever seriously a question of creating them? Not so far as is known. A few more or less discrete allusions to the opposition of one country or another appeared in the press. After the Moscow conference in April, 1947, it was learned that there was a break between the U.S.S.R. and the Western powers. In June, 1948, the division of Germany into two parts, eastern and western, would be marked by the creation of the *Deutschemark*.

The conclusion was reached that settlement was impossible. Yet almost three years had elapsed since Potsdam; it is not three years after date that a treaty should be applied. Why were the economics affairs ministries not organized within three months, as they could and should have been? If the Westerners had insisted then with the Soviets, is it certain that the latter would have declined to carry out an important clause of the treaty they had just concluded? They were not yet as established in their zone as they would be later; they did not yet have the desire or the will to remain there, as they would later after a long occupation. Had they refused, the cosigners could have renounced the whole treaty. And Moscow did not yet have atomic weapons, the American and British forces were not demobilized, Czechoslovakia and China were not yet communist. Nothing proves that Stalin would have vetoed the project for a united Germany; in fact,

France and Germany

Germany was not yet split, but was simply divided into occupation zones, as Austria was.

If these zones had been adhered to, across which the Germany ministries would have managed the country's economy, as the Austrian ministries were doing in Austria. it would not have been possible to establish one coinage on one side, another on the other, a communist system in the East, a capitalistic system in the West. Germany would have remained a whole, and when the occupation ended, she would have had a German government, which would have signed a peace treaty with the occupying forces. We can suppose that the latter would have let the Germans choose their political regime, as they did for the Italians and the Austrians. No doubt they would have imposed certain military conditions on the Germans, such as disarmament or limited rearmament, as well as a position of neutrality, at least temporarily. No doubt, the Western powers and the Soviets would have sought later on, each on his own, to attract this Germany to their side, but she would not have been cut in two, as she is today.

When the Western powers congratulate themselves on having Germany in their camp (three-fourths of the Germans, that is), one wonders if they don't prefer this solution to the more natural one, out of which a more pacific Europe might have been born.

The Germans, for their part—at the very least those of the west—have played the Western game to the limit and have never sought to modify it or even influence it; not that they have not deplored the division of their country, but it seems that fear of communism has paralyzed them. This fear

224

has caused them to reject all contact with Moscow, and particularly with their eastern compatriots. They have enjoyed repeating that their unification was not their business, but that of the occupying forces, and as the latter did little to advance the matter (perhaps they could do no more than they did), the Germans were patient.

Germany's policy and that of the Allies is henceforth a fact we must accept, since it is at the base of the present situation. On the German side there was an immediate acceptance of it. It was understood that although France was not the motive force in the Western alliance, she was an essential part of it, precisely because of her long Franco–German difficulties. In any case, an end had to be made to that. Two great neighboring countries cannot quarrel indefinitely. Why should the circumstances which imposed this rapprochement not have been welcomed? We are generally happy over those constraints which remove all pretext of refusing what we really want in our heart.

It might be said that understanding with France was advocated in Germany almost without opposition; the alliance was a natural result. Instances of resistance appeared concerning particular disputes, such as that of the Saar. In such a case, can it be required that a nation give up its own interests in favor of a partner? If the desire for an understanding is in proportion to good will, then good will was never lacking in the German leaders since the rise to power of Chancellor Adenauer, whose spirit of conciliation was truly exemplary.

France and Germany

More complex was France's attitude; the country was more divided, more hesitant. Its governments, less stable, had not always followed the same line. Certain of them had thought they should return to the old policy of dividing Germany—the demand for separation of the Ruhr, the refusal to establish the economic ministries provided for all Germany by the Potsdam agreements. Robert Schuman had the good sense and the courage to reverse this policy. However, the military alliance could go beyond his intentions.

Rapprochement with an armed Germany was less popular than with an unarmed Germany. It touched a sensitive spot, and clashed with old habits. It was different with the English and the Americans, since affinities have always united them with the Germans. The Anglo–Saxon mistrusted Soviet Russia; they had no more hostility toward conquered Germany, from which the Nazi virus seemed to have been removed. If they had twice gone to war against Germany, it was because she was troublesome and dangerous to them, but henceforth the danger came from another quarter, and since the new Germany was democratic, London and Washington found that she had the qualifications for admission to their camp.

For the French, however, she remained more or less the hereditary enemy, and the idea of introducing her into the Atlantic alliance made public opinion bristle. The idea came from America, which had proposed it at the time of the Korean War, in order to strengthen the Atlantic alliance. Caught short, French statesmen had given proof of skill and wisdom; they wanted to safeguard relations with Germany as well as with France's allies, and the latter all supported German rearmament. A compromise was suggested: the European army. Germany would not have her autonomous army; her forces would be integrated with those of five other European countries. Thus deprived of independent direction, without freedom of movement, controlled as much as possible, the German army would be less to be feared and it would help make European ties closer.

Whatever we think of this formula, which could have had its inconveniences and which was rejected, we must agree that it had attractive aspects, corresponding to solid realities. In the last two wars the combatant armies never showed the same hostility toward each other that was displayed by home front civilians. Participating in the same life and the same perils, the men who faced each other were capable of understanding and esteeming each other. Soldiers of all countries have the same training, the same mentality; the same courage and discipline are required of them. In no other profession, no other trade group, are men of different nations closer to one another than career military men. It can be supposed that they would have got along without difficulty in a common army.

Everyone will admit that two peoples obliged to come together to defend themselves, to prepare together for a possible conflict, can only draw from this togetherness the feeling of a common destiny, and therefore feel closer to each other. If it were not that way, when a common danger threatens them, there would be a disturbing disparity between them. Would French soldiers be willing to fight on the Elbe or the Oder to serve as a shield for unarmed Germans? Wouldn't it be humiliating for the German people, going about its business as usual, while foreigners would be taking their place on the front line? There can be no friendship and esteem without common sacrifices. An entente between France and Germany could not be limited to an exchange of goods, tourists, and orchestra leaders. As long as the world situation requires soldiers, both countries must be ready to furnish them, to have them serve side by side.

Although reversals of alliances in the past sought diplomatic and military objectives, such as opposing a coalition, in peace as in war, the reversal which put France at Germany's side had a larger meaning; two peoples, long enemies, understood that they must become reconciled. They had already made certain gestures which augured well, but which were of little consequence. It was only by pooling their arms that they would prove to others and to themselves that they no longer wanted to bear them against each other, but to fight for the same cause.

The abandonment of the European Defense Community, after the long period of time spent in establishing it, may or may not be regrettable; although we do not know what its practical results might have been, it is certain that for four years France was a spectacle of irritating uncertainty. There was a policy different from that of the Defense Community which could have been adopted and should have been proposed in its place: if France was really hostile to German rearmament, why didn't she play that card all the way, by relying on the majority of the Germans, who were no less opposed to it? Here there was a singular accord between the two peoples, and it might have served as the basis for a policy.

However, the rejection of the European Defense Community showed that French public opinion was not ripe for *that kind of policy,* even between an armed France and an unarmed Germany. To draw close to Germany without reference to America was to go further than Robert Schuman himself was going, and might have meant the isolation of Germany and France. There was evidently no one in France who would have dared attempt it, and it is not certain either that Germany would have accepted this close relationship.

France therefore finally resigned herself to the reversal of alliances, becoming the ally of a Germany provided with an autonomous army in the Atlantic structure—in other words, a military alliance of classic type, the kind of thing she had at first rejected. The limitations imposed on Germany were insignificant and unguaranteed. The Atlantic pact set minima, not maxima, for its participants. How in the long run, could a maximum limit of armament or even a prohibition of atomic weapons be imposed on Germany?

An autonomous army permits German policy to adapt someday to different circumstances, which are already foreseen: reunification, fusion of West Germany with East Germany. Germany will be able to negotiate this more freely than if her army belonged to a European army. She will be able to utilize the army for interior purposes, for example, to prevent communism from overflowing into her territory when the communist elements of the eastern part are integrated into a united Germany.

It is difficult to say whether this independence granted to the army and consequently to German policy is good or bad. There are Germans who would have preferred a European army to establish their country's policy more firmly. We can nevertheless admit that if certain particular tasks became incumbent upon Germany, it is not necessary that her allies be concerned in them. Up to now she has not misused her relative military freedom; she has slowed down rearmament and has reduced the number of troops she was originally to put under arms. She is keeping well within the limits of the role which was prescribed for her.

Whatever we think of her status, of her future military power, it appears difficult today to desire her demilitarization. The time when she could have been disarmed has gone by; the world situation will not permit a great people to live unarmed at the center of Europe. Even if some day she should be neutralized, Germany needs a shield for herself and for Europe, and Frances's own security requires it.[120]

The reversal of alliances which finally put Germany in the Western camp ended the absurd alliance with Russia which, after splitting Europe apart, handed two-thirds of it over to communism. There are nevertheless Frenchmen who still have a nostalgic longing for this alliance. Tradition dictates that in Paris a wall shall separate domestic policy from foreign policy. It isn't considered very important that Germany has adopted democracy in the occidental mode; people do not always measure the extent of the upheaval that the alliance of Russian communism with Russian imperialism has brought into world politics. People ask why the new Germany does not come to an understanding with the U.S.S.R., as the Third Republic did with the czar, as Hitler did with Stalin? Why shouldn't France, today or tomorrow, as yesterday, vie with Germany for the alliance with Russia? There's nothing to create opposition between France and the U.S.S.R. (nothing except communism, a mere trifle!); they have no common boundary or any territorial disputes. The U.S.S.R. and the United States don't have any, either—and they have the advantage which France does not, of being so far from each other that only certain weapons can reach them. Soviet armies, tanks, motorized units, parachutists, and so on are a few hours' march from France. They wouldn't even need to enter France; all they would need to do is to reach her eastern border for the pro-Moscow party to rise to power. Germany's fate would decide that of France. The two countries are indissolubly linked; when the Russians reach the Rhine, whether as allies of Germany or after they have defeated her, France's fate will have been settled.

More logical and more clairvoyant than some Frenchmen, the Soviet leaders themselves denounced the "beautiful and good alliance" of 1944. They did not agree that people can be friends and enemies at the same time. The Franco–Soviet alliance had been concluded against Germany before the war was over, and from the day that France and Germany joined the Atlantic alliance oriented against the U.S.S.R., this treaty was evidently null and void. The same would hold even if the Atlantic alliance should disappear—an anti-communist France cannot be the ally of a communist Russia, so long as there is no peril greater than communism. At the very most she can have correct, perhaps even cordial relations with her, from people to people, and not just from power to power, as with Yugoslavia and Poland.

People like to think of the old Franco–Russian alliance as a traditional alliance; it lived no more than a quarter-century, from the military convention of 1892 to the October revolution of 1917. Although there have been relatively few periods of hostility between Russia and France (Napoleon's campaign of 1812, and the Crimean War in 1856 are the exceptions), Russia's policy toward France has never been anything except the exploiting of France's strength and weakness. In 1871 the czar's government took advantage of the German victory over France to escape from the clauses of the treaty of Paris which prohibited her from having a fleet on the Black Sea. In 1872 Russia signed with the emperors of Germany and Austria the alliance called "The League of the Three Emperors." Four years later, she proposed alliance to Bismarck, and it was only after he had refused, when Balkan policy set Russia against Austria–Hungary, which was supported by Germany, that Russia would ally herself with France. She would then help herself liberally to French savings, and the loans would never be repaid.

This faithful ally drew France into two world wars.[121] It was not over such Franco–German disputes as Alsace–Lorraine or Morocco that the first one broke out, but over a Russo–German quarrel. In that war, Russia abandoned her Western allies, and they would have had difficulty in winning if America had not intervened. The Second World War was touched off by the Hitler–Stalin accord of August 23, 1939, after France and England, in a six months' negotiation, had tried in vain to come to an agreement with the Soviet government against Germany. Stalin hoped that a long campaign in the west would wear out both the French and the German forces and that he would remain master of the situation. In 1940, he congratulated Hitler on his victory over France. At the war's end, he would oppose France's having a zone of occupation, and her presence in various international meetings.

After an experience of that kind, how is it possible to have a weakness for the largest and most imperialistic power in the world, as if that power could have any aim other than to add France to her satellites and utilize her for her own ends? The first effect of an alliance with Russia would be to turn the United States, England, and all Western Europe against France, in other words, to proscribe France in that part of the world—a pleasant prospect for those French whose ideal is not yet Marx, Lenin, and Khrushchev!

These French Russophiles, haunted by the old political-strategic maneuver which consisted of taking Germany from behind, forget that this Germany is not a great power today, and neither is France. Neither has any chance of becoming a big power again, and the danger which threatens them is to be overrun, absorbed, or at the very least, dominated by Soviet Russia. A Franco–Russian alliance against Germany would have the same results as a German–Russian alliance against France—in either case, Germany and France would both be conquered and enslaved by the U.S.S.R. Her victory would imply their immediate Sovietization and that of the whole European continent as well.

233

France's interest, and Germany's too, excludes the alliance with Russia for both of them, and the only recourse the two peoples have is to draw together against the threat which hangs over them. The reversal of alliances was written into the total victory of Soviet Russia, a victory which made her a world power, as dangerous for France as she is for Germany. Even if there had been no Atlantic pact, the two former enemies would have had to draw closer together to defend themselves.[122]

[117]Roosevelt, whose capitulations to Stalin at Teheran and Yalta have been criticized, had proposed not to establish separate occupation zones, but to place Germany under a central government of the four occupying powers, with their troops distributed over the whole country. Such a solution does not appear to have been impossible, and it might have prevented the division of Germany. After some time, the inter-Allied government would quite naturally have been replaced by a German government, and not by two different and hostile German governments.

[118]Mirabeau to the Duke de Lauzun: "We are divided between the land and the sea. Where are we going? To gather the bitter fruits of universal mistrust, to fall in complete exhaustion in trying to force the nature of things, which does not allow a single power to wield two scepters." (July 21, 1786)

Talleyrand, friendly with Mirabeau at the time, prided himself on having first had the idea of the Franco–British alliance.

[119]The accord provided for "departments necessary for finances, transportation, communication, foreign trade, and industry."

[120]The Soviets themselves did not demand the total disarmament of Germany. Some of their leaders stated that they would agree to an army of 100,000 men, such as the Treaty of Versailles had specified; but today, an army of that size, provided with atomic weapons, cannot be compared with one of the same size at the time of Versailles.

234

Did they understand in Moscow that a great people cannot be disarmed, unless it is for a short time, immediately following a defeat?

[121]We might add that during the first war, Russia demanded that France and England, in the event of a victory, hand over all of Poland. Poland owed its resurrection in 1918 only to the simultaneous or successive defeats of Russia, Germany, and Austria–Hungary. If the Triple Entente, including czarist Russia, had won the war, it is probable that Poland would have fallen under the yoke of Russia . . . where she is today.

[122]This necessity could be relaxed only if the combination of circumstances were profoundly modified. If, for instance, Germany became completely reunified and drew closer to Poland. For that to happen, it would be necessary, not only that the U.S.S.R., opposed to German unity, should reverse its attitude, but that Poland should draw away from her. It would be also necessary that Poland and Germany reach an agreement on their common boundary.

Another possibility would be that the communist regime might undergo a profound transformation inside the U.S.S.R. and its satellites, that it might evolve, for example, in the direction of Yugoslavian communism, taking on a different form in each country and abandoning all imperialism, all propaganda in foreign countries, or, another possibility, that an effective reduction of tensions be produced between east and west.

In that case, France and Germany, without allying themselves to the U.S.S.R., would not have the same need to ally themselves against her.

As for the desire to trade with the east, which perhaps might bring Germany closer to Moscow, it can be found in Germany as in other countries. To what extent is it feasible today? Certain German industrialists are cited—and they admit it openly—who would like to place their goods in communist countries. But any important trade requires a corresponding activity, and the products which the U.S.S.R. and her satellites can send to Germany are for the moment few in number. It is not exchanges of these kinds which threaten to reverse German policy.

CHAPTER 20

Europe and The Holy Empire

THE union of France and Germany within the Atlantic structure does not exhaust the possibilities of French–German policy. This union began at almost the same time in another structure, that of Europe, which at first had no military aspects. It was primarily economic, but also cultural and political. When the attempt to create a European army and a supranational political authority failed, the idea of an economic community, considered to be the most fertile possibility for the moment, was retained.

It was France which advocated the idea of a European organization, taking up again one of Briand's ideas which had not been followed through; we noted above that Stresemann had criticized his conception, since the German minister put economics in first place. Obviously, Robert Schumann and

Jean Monnet were following in his footsteps when they launched the European Coal and Steel Community, the first of the European institutions; it was limited to coal and steel, but it would be followed by the Common Market.

It has been observed that France was less inclined than Germany toward European establishments. There are many reasons for this; first of all, there are reasons of a historical nature: Germany preserves the tradition of the Holy Empire, which helps her accept the plans for European union. The Germans are consequently better prepared for union than the French, whose tradition is a strictly national one. It has been claimed that Europe would be, for the Germans, according to this tradition, merely a camouflage for German domination of the other nations. Such an ambition might be one of the projects of a Hitler, but never did the Holy Empire dominate or aspire to dominate Europe.

A great symbol without being a great power

Seen in modern perspective, the Holy Roman Germanic Empire seems to have been a failure, perhaps the great failure of German history. It was, writes the eminent Belgian historian Henri Pirenne, "a misfortune for Europe and Germany. Europe did not become the Christian republic it could have been, and Germany exhausted herself by trying to keep Italy under her yoke."[123] In pursuing the unfulfilled dream of the supranational state, she failed for several centuries to obtain her own national unity. A number of Germans do not accept this opinion. We should perhaps not be surprised that they still admire the Holy Empire, that imposing edifice which had endured longer than the Roman Empire. A phenomenon of this importance cannot be judged exclusively from the modern point of view. We have to put ourselves in the place of the contemporaries and the actors of a history which lasted for 844 years.[124]

People sometimes like to confuse the Holy Empire and the empire of Charlemagne, which never bore that name; it was known as the "Western Empire." The earlier one can be considered as the first version of the second, or the second as its successor. Is there any continuity between the two? It can be said that there is, since more or less obscure personages continued to attribute the title of emperor to themselves.[125] But that is of little importance. There is a great deal of difference between the empire of Charlemagne and the Holy Empire; the first included France, which never belonged to the second. The association of France and Germany was the fundamental characteristic of Charlemagne's empire; it gave it a double base which could have assured its strength, if the emperor's grandsons had not destroyed it by dividing it. The Holy Empire lacked this foundation and was never a strong construction. The Franco–German Empire covered Western and Central Europe, it was capable of extending to the west toward England and Spain, to the east toward the Oder and along the Danube. Separated from France, which was to quarrel with it over the median strip of Lotharingia, exhausting itself in interminable quarrels with the pope and the Italian city-states, the German Empire owed to its central position the fact that it was surrounded by enemies who at first halted its expansion, then encroached upon its territory.

The emperors thought they could associate their temporal power with the spiritual power of the Church. This dividing up the empire of souls and that of bodies was based on an illusion, that of the parallel sovereignties, which were supposed to be exercised in a perfect harmony in two separate domains. They were not so distinct as one might think. There were points of contention, such as the appointing of bishops, and the thought in the back of the emperor's mind was to dominate the pope, just as the pope's idea was to dominate the emperor. In reality, two powerful wills were opposing each other, and the pope's, more flexible, more difficult to fathom, extending as it did over the whole occidental world, eventually won.

During the Middle Ages there was, however, in men's minds an idea of the Holy Empire as a supranational power. We find it in Italians like Dante; a partisan of the German emperor, he did not hesitate to place Hugh Capet in his Inferno, since the king of France was for him the empire's mortal enemy, seeking to carve out his state in the body of Christendom. It was the emperor who personified Christendom and who wanted to make peace rule in it, whereas the king's aim was power. Here, the poet was idealizing—he did not see that all wanted power, the emperor, the popes, and the Capetian king.

If we think of the fact that an emperor like Frederick II, contemporary of Saint Louis, born in Italy, calling himself Caesar of Rome, of Italy, of Sicily, of Jerusalem, and of

Arles, made only infrequent appearances inside Germany, we will understand the extent to which the Germans were hypnotized by a country which was for them the imperial land par excellence. In that century the empire was called simply, "Roman"; the epithet "germanic" would not be added until the end of the fifteenth century; it would have scandalized emperors like the Hohenstaufens, who preferred Italy to Germany. This preference, the long periods of absence which were its result, no doubt also the electoral character of the empire and the particularism of the German princes caused the emperors to lose all power and left them with only a simple title—a title which, it is true, was brilliant and coveted and which the greatest families fought over, until the day when the Hapsburgs succeeded in implanting it in their family.

They remedied the weakness of the emperor in Germany by displacing the center of their power, which henceforth would be in their personal domains, outside Germany, except for Austria. This meant that the concept of the Holy Empire had already disappeared, replaced with the concept of a dynasty which, like all the dynasties of the time, sought to aggrandize itself by all possible means, and to fortify its prestige. It succeeded only with great difficulty, having to fight against the political and geographic constitution of an empire which was dispersed and disunited. Its greatest emperor, Charles V, would have to divide it before his death between his brother and his son. The Hapsburgs of Vienna and those of Madrid would not even be able to maintain themselves by association. The Spanish branch would be elimi-

nated by the Bourbons, the Austrian branch by Protestantism, by the blows struck against it by Richelieu, Louis XIV,
and Napoleon, and by the rise of a new German power,
Prussia.

Isn't it tragic that this dynasty, capable of being supported by a great people like the Germans, joining lesser peoples to it, such as the Dutch, the Czechs, the Hungarians, succeeded neither in founding a national German state nor a
more or less supranational federative state, of which Germans
would have formed the core, and all of whose members would
have enjoyed a more or less generous autonomy? This is what
Switzerland was able to achieve on a smaller scale, Russia
on a much larger one.[126]

With a very long delay in comparison to other national
states, the German national state was finally created by Prussia, but without German Austria. This little kernel remained
within the old empire, which was becoming Slavic, but
it could not prevent it from crumbling away.

The Holy Empire had played an important role in the
Middle Ages. Its place, unique in the Western world, did
not depend on a power which belonged only to the first emperors. The empire maintained for a long time in Europe an
idea of unity which eventually weakened, but at the same
time, it represented the fusion of people's faith in the Christian world and the continuity of Roman administration and
law, two great ideas which came from Rome and the Church.
Its defect lay in the fact that its roots were only in
men's minds. It was never a military power—and the absence
of real power prevented it from accomplishing what its task

241

should have been, that of international arbitration. "Europe," Henri Pirenne writes, "admitted that it had a sovereign arbiter above the individual kings.[127] The notion that the Roman Empire could become a German empire could not have occurred to anyone; far from Germany's having sacrificed the empire for its own profit, Germany's kings sacrificed her to their universal role. It turned them away from national politics, orienting them toward a grandiose and inaccessible goal."

Voltaire's quip is well known: "The Holy Roman Germanic Empire, which is neither holy, nor Roman, nor Germanic . . ." This is hardly a joke; if the Holy Empire ceased to be Roman without becoming German, wasn't that the reason why it could not establish a durable and strong German state?

Memory of the empire explains the nostalgia which persists among the Germans. We wonder if they see the reasons for its failure. It is, of course, understandable that an attempt, even a simple one, to unify Europe along spiritual and temporal lines makes an impression on certain minds, and that in the presence of the new idea of Europe, the Germans are more receptive than other peoples. We find this same feeling in Austria, Belgium, the Netherlands, and Luxembourg, countries which belonged for a long time to the Holy Empire. It is less evident among the Swiss, who separated from it earlier.

Was the Holy Empire the shield of Europe?

One function which the panegyrists of the Holy Empire readily attribute to it is that of protector of Europe against the invasions from the east. In the days of Attila, weren't the

Franks and the Goths, at the side of the Roman Aetius, to drive back the Huns who had invaded the north of France? Charles Martel halted the Arabs at Poitiers; he and his soldiers were Franks, also known as Germans. In the tenth century the Hungarians, advancing into central Europe, were defeated by Henry I, king of Germany, later Emperor Otto. In the thirteenth century, the Mongols invaded Germany, Poland, Hungary, defeated the army of the Crusaders near Tokay, and massacred the French Templars; again it was German forces which stopped them at Wahlstatt and at Olmütz.

It was particularly in the seventeenth century, at the time of the Turkish advance on Vienna, that the empire is said to have saved Christian Europe from oriental infidels. It was said that Louis XIV paid the Sultan to besiege the imperial capital; but hadn't Francis I already concluded an alliance with Soliman II? Didn't the kings of France show that they were ready to sacrifice the defense of Europe to their personal glory, whereas the Germans were raising a barrier against the invaders from the east?

There is much to be said about this interpretation of history. The Franks who fought against Attila or at Poitiers were not the Holy Empire. It was, in a general way the Germanic peoples who created an obstacle to the eastern invasions, but it was for geographic reasons—they happened to be in the east, in the vanguard of occidental peoples and were first to be attacked. Each, in those days, defended himself as best he could, without thinking about protecting those behind him.

It has been said but not proved that Charlemagne, emperor of the West, may have sought an alliance with the Moslem Haroun-al-Raschid against the Byzantine emperor. In any case, the French participated in the Crusades with the Germans and even played a great role in them. In the sixteenth century, when Francis I opened relations with Soliman, the notion of Christendom was already greatly weakened, and the blows struck by the German Luther against the Holy Empire were fatal in a different way from the attacks of the Turks. The latter, even if they had taken Vienna, were not strong enough to conquer Germany. We must agree nevertheless that the Turkish alliance was not indispensable for Louis XIV, who had nothing to fear from the emperor.

Later, Germany would not contribute with England and France to the liberation of the Greeks from these same Turks; at the beginning of the twentieth century, Germany and Austria–Hungary openly sided with them against the small Balkan nations. The truth is that never did a European nation hesitate to ally itself with Asiatics against other Europeans. We have only recently come to realize that that is one of the causes of the decadence of Europe.

The real "eastern peril" is of recent date. An aftermath of Hitler's offensive against the Slavs, it results from the fact that Russia, the great Slav state, joining the West against Germany, was able to advance into the heartland of Europe, then to make an alliance with the largest Asiatic people, the Chinese. And there we have a combination of circumstances which had never appeared in the time of the Holy Empire, when Russia was trying to extend eastward to Asia and the

Pacific. Weren't the Russians, who for more than two centuries were under Mongol rule,[128] the vanguard then of Europe against Asia, living on good terms with the German rulers, and with the emperor and the king of Prussia as well? But times have changed ...

France, Germany, Europe

It is not a question of seeking inspiration today in the Holy Empire as a model, but we do need to draw a lesson from it. First of all, there are certain broad lines to be noted:

(1) Unlike the Holy Empire, the new Europe must not be impotent; it must have economic and military power. The first of these did not have so much importance in the past, but today it is the very condition of the second. And the second one is indispensable. Europe—except in the case of disarmament which at present appears unlikely—needs atomic weapons as well as the so-called traditional weapons, even if they are never to be used. For the time being, Europe's armed force cannot be autonomous; without American help, it would not be capable of fighting or of having its neutrality respected, if it wanted to remain neutral.

(2) What gave the Holy Empire its prestige—its original alliance with the Church and its claim of continuing the Roman Empire—is henceforth no longer a factor. Europe is no longer a Catholic community; it contains Catholics, Protestants, and free thinkers. Its churches are independent of the states, and they will maintain good relations with the European organization to the extent to which they will support it with their authority.

(3) It is unthinkable that a hereditary or elected leader should be at the head of this Europe. Whatever the acceptable formula may be, it can be only a federation, an association similar to the Commonwealth without supranational authority, or perhaps on the contrary, provided with that kind of authority. The choice of one or the other of these formulae is not without importance, but it may depend on circumstances.

(4) What is to be the extent of this Europe? Some insist that it include England, which has long been reticent about it; others would carry it to the Urals, which is not an international border. The U.S.S.R. extends to the Pacific; she is both European and Asiatic and could not be cut in two in order to bring one part into Europe. As for England, although her intentions are better today than they were some years ago, we will have to show patience and flexibility with her, and grant her special concessions at the beginning, since her empirical nature finds ready-made structures repugnant.

The eastern European countries will also belong to the European union, when they have ceased to be satellites of the U.S.S.R. It is to be feared that this is far in the future. If we hold for the time being to the Europe called the Europe of the Six, or of the Seven (with Great Britain), or of the Seventeen (with the other members of the OCDE), this is because it alone shows a beginning of practical accomplishment. It is no ideal, but it is a starting point. It matters little whether the European organization includes at first six, ten, fifteen, or more nations. Even if there were only two at least that would be something. Europe will be created by stages, and those who are hesitant now will rally in the future if they see results.

Moreover, it is true that Europe is developing on different planes, with different participants. There are six member states in the European Coal and Steel Community and the Common Market, fifteen on the Strasbourg Council, while the OCDE includes seventeen. This evolution seems due to continue; the atomic community is being established both on the plane of the six and on a larger plane. The Common Market could be enlarged by the addition of the "Seven," England and six other countries being linked by a "free exchange zone." All of this appears a bit chaotic, but how can it be otherwise when the new Europe is not being born of one political domination or of the preponderance of one country or of one dictator like Napoleon or Hitler, a situation no one desires.

At present, European plans are being oriented along the lines of the Common Market and Euratom—in other words, along economic lines. Nevertheless, political union seems no less necessary, and might perhaps be easier to achieve. Recent events have shown that European nations, already reduced to satellite rank, will descend to that of vassals if they do not have a common policy in the face of major world events. Lacking a developed organization (supranational government and parliament), they appear, to begin with, to be satisfied with periodic meetings of heads of government and principal ministers. There would be discussion of current problems and points of view would be compared. Normally a unanimous decision should be reached, rather than decisions by the majority, as in the United Nations, which are annulled by the veto power. Such an accord is always possible among a small group of nations whose relations are based on a fundamental understanding. Their differences, which must be minimal, can always be set aside by friendly debate and mutual concessions. Such an innovation seems much simpler. Even with European institutions having precisely defined powers, it could be set up as rapidly as the economic union, which involves complex interests and requires a detailed organization. Its complete establishment appears feasible in about fifteen years, but can, of course, be speeded up.

In the European structure, Franco–German relations are of capital importance, not only because of the size and importance of the countries but also because they must influence others. England is scarcely less essential, but she has always been reluctant; her problems are peculiar to her and they will require special solutions. It is only gradually that she will consent, if she ever does, to a total integration to which the Commonwealth is perhaps less opposed than we think.

One wonders if there is any logical basis to the often expressed idea that the British counterweight would be useful or even necessary to prevent Germany from dominating Europe. Certainly England's presence is desirable, because one of the principal European powers must not remain outside Europe, but there are no more chances of seeing her always on France's side against Germany than of seeing Germany always on France's side against England. England's European interests do not coincide any more with those of France than with those of Germany.[129] Nor would it be a matter, for France, of allying herself on such and such an issue with Italy against Germany, or with Germany against Italy. Some people think of European union as a parliamentary regime in which nations, replacing parties, would oppose each other. Perhaps there would be something similar in an international parliament, but the blocs would not always be formed according to nations, but also according to parties, socialists against conservatives or liberals. So long as we are in the stage of consultation and agreements among governments, we repeat, the decisions will be based on conciliation rather than on majority votes.

The same will be true in the economic field. Once the Common Market is established after free negotiations, why fear a German "hegemony"? It has never frightened such small countries as Belgium, Holland, or Luxembourg. The economic field, except for unusual cases originating in politics, is not one of hegemony, but of competition.[130] A small country, if its products are cheap and of good quality, competes successfully with the largest one. Switzerland controls the watch-making trade because she is better at it than the others; the United States has to defend itself against her by high tariffs. Can it be said that Switzerland is exercising a hegemony, as if there were an imperialism in watches? Anyone can vie with her for first place, provided he does a better job.[131]

Are we to think, along with certain nationalists, that European integration would be harmful to national groups? If we stop to think that since the establishment of easier means of transportation, beginning with the railroads, the

French have traveled much more—government employees, soldiers, business men, and tourists move constantly from one province to another, marriages are increasing between men and women from different provinces, and that nevertheless, Normandy is still Normandy, Provence is Provence, we must admit that among countries separated by a language barrier, such as France, Italy, or Germany, relations will always be less intimate than among provinces of the same country, and that, as a result, an excessive mixing of populations, a leveling out of national characters, does not appear likely. The leveling which is being produced not only in Europe but all over the world passes over international boundaries and customs barriers. It is the result of radio, movies, television, the automobile, the airplane, sports, and travel, distributing the same pictures, the same sounds, the same names of stars and the same customs everywhere.

One important detail, still being discussed, is the relations of Europe with America. There have been up to now in France and in Germany partisans of the Atlantic pact who are hostile toward European union; they feel that the European nations would have an advantage in coming to an understanding with the United States separately rather than among themselves. Don't accidents like that of Suez condemn this thesis? Two European powers, England and France, found themselves obliged to suspend, upon a sign from Washington, an action which had been closely planned in common. Would it be the same if all the Europeans formed a bloc? In some cases, perhaps. But a bloc of two hundred million persons could always make itself heard better than divided nations.

The European nations which are members of NATO have tried to obtain within this organization, military up to now, a political coordination which they should first establish among themselves. Weren't they putting the cart before the horse? America refused the invitation, arguing that she had numerous interests in the world outside the Atlantic alliance. Why, indeed, should Germany, France, or Belgium be concerned with Formosa, the Philippines, or Alaska? But if the United States had accepted consultations with its allies on all these problems, each one acting for itself and pulling in its own direction, would the Europeans ever have counterbalanced American mass and power? It is not very likely. In order for there to be a certain equality in the Atlantic organization, Europe must represent a certain strength.

In fact, the states of Europe are faced with this alternative: to unite and become a great power, politically and economically, or to remain what they are—individually associated with America, which is the same thing as accentuating and making definitive the position they already have as satellites, and at the risk of someday seeing the United States and the U.S.S.R. reaching an understanding over their heads.

Does German unity threaten Europe?

Although it has been talked of for years, we see less and less how Germany's reunification could occur, and the Germans, reasonably enough, are growing impatient. They had the illusion along with the Allies, that Western pressure would finally cause the U.S.S.R. to give up its occupation zone and consent to free elections. Elections could be only a resounding slap in the face for Soviet Russia, re-echoing throughout the satellites; she will never agree to them. In addition, it is not known if she intends to rebuild the zone she occupies. She hopes perhaps to Sovietize it indefinitely, to make of it a people's republic which would remain forever separated from West Germany. The most likely possibility is that she will seek to keep it as long as possible, and will give it up only for a definite advantage. This is what the Germans mean by their realistic saying, "There will be a price."

But what could the price be? Who will pay it? The Western allies have little to offer. The U.S.S.R. claims that it fears the atomic arming of Germany, which will of necessity be limited. Today it is the U.S.S.R. herself who is ahead and she has every chance of keeping the lead. It is conceivable that the price could be a security agreement covering all Europe, but it would be of little value; no one has ever taken such agreements seriously, the U.S.S.R. less than anyone else. Or she might ask for the withdrawal of Western troops from Germany and the neutralization of certain zones, which would be possible; at the very least, it might be the departure of the Anglo–French–American garrisons, but that would not be enough for Moscow. We might also think of the possibility of economic assistance, but this is less and less necessary to the U.S.S.R., as her production and standard of living rise. The Soviets will not let East Germany go for a few dollars, and what is true for the Western allies taken as a bloc naturally applies to France. Could she do any more than the others to help Germany toward reunification? Perhaps unexpected opportunities will appear someday, but we do not see them at the moment.

Who can propose anything like the withdrawal of Germany from the Atlantic alliance, or her neutralization, or the limitation or suppression of her armed forces? Only Germany herself could make such concessions. It isn't certain that they would be enough but they would establish a good basis for discussion. It might be that the U.S.S.R. would also demand a special status for East Germany, which, although reintegrated into the larger German state, would preserve certain social and economic institutions imposed by Moscow. This would be a difficult point; the events of 1956 in Poland and in Hungary lead one to believe that such a regime would not long endure in one-fourth of Germany, with the other three-fourths opposed to it.

We cannot dwell too long on a problem which is essentially up to the Germans. It is clear that the Western powers will have something to say in it, since the reunification might affect their relations with Germany. We can even suppose that the latter would act in agreement with them. Even if the conditions of reunification were not of a nature to please them, could they refuse to bow to necessity? If they are not capable of solving a problem which is essential to them, to Europe and to the world, can they prevent the principal interested party from solving it himself?

Here any prognostic would be pointless. The reunification can occur in an unforeseen way at an unexpected moment. It is probable that it will occur by evolution, if tension is reduced between east and west, and if the Germans increase contacts between the two Germanys. For the present, the West Germans find this repugnant, either because they refuse to recognize the government of East Germany, or because they fear communist propaganda in the Federal Republic. These contacts, and the means of developing relations between the two Germanys are their concern along.

Some Europeans, although they make a point of saying that they favor a reunification which is in the order of things are really fundamentally opposed to it; they fear that it will be harmful to European union. This fear is not without justification, and it might be supposed that a united Europe would be less threatened in a few years than it is now, if this union were to be considered then. Yet we must tell ourselves that such considerations would not stop the Germans. Whatever may be the moment when circumstances will allow them to unify their country, they will not hesitate to do it, whatever their attachments. Nothing else can count in the eyes of a people which has lost half its territory, when one-fourth appears lost forever, and the possibility occurs of recovering the other fourth. For Europe, if association with Germany could not be maintained under the same conditions, the question would then be to seek new conditions.

Whatever happens, it is not to be feared that Germany will abandon Europe. Political association, penetration, even fusion of economies, if it is possible someday—all are desirable, but European peoples are also joined by their spirit, their common past, and their common ideas. In this respect, Germany has always belonged to Europe and she will certainly not reject it. Her aversion for totalitarian regimes, the doctrines of which she has at times produced, which she has had to suffer and which she knows better than anyone else, places her in the group of the free nations. This classification cannot be questioned again.

The Holy Empire is a thing of the past; the Europe which is now in gestation will not be very much like it. At least it will preserve a little of its spirit. France, Germany, and the other nations who will contribute to its creation will have to pursue this task with more conscience and strength than could be done in past centuries, when the aspirations of peoples were obscured by dynastic ambitions. This conscience and this strength will be absolutely necessary to protect Europe against ideologies which are conquering a large part of the world.

[123]From Henri Pirenne, *L'Allemagne moderne et l'empire romain du Moyen Age.* Pirenne's observation is all the more noteworthy because the tradition of the Holy Empire still lives on in Belgium, a country which belonged to it for centuries. All it takes to ascertain this is to go through any manual of history written for Belgian school children, where one may read that Charles V was Belgian, the authors not hesitating to side with him in his fight against France.

[124]From 962, the date when Otto I, the king of Germany, was crowned emperor by the pope, to 1806, when Francis II, under pressure from Napoleon, substituted the name of Empire of Austria for that of Holy Roman Germanic Empire. In German, the latter was called *Heiliges Römisches Reich Deutscher Nation,* or "Holy Roman Empire of the German Nation."

[125]From the Carolingian Charles the Fat, the imperial title passed to Italians, Guy of Spoleto and his son, Lambert. It returned to Arnulf, next to last of the eastern Carolingians, then passed to the king of Provence, Louis III, then to various

Italians. For nearly a century, it was a disputed title, although it corresponded to nothing real. Can there be an emperor without an empire?

[126]Of course, Russia is federalist only in appearance, the Russians dominating the other peoples in it. Yet in a multi-national state all gradations are permitted between the total autonomy of the nationalities and the supremacy of a single people as in the Roman Empire. In the possible association of the Germans and several other peoples, the Germans were numerous enough to have retained control without using constraint.

[127]Certain emperors had a try at this arbiter's role. For example, Sigismund went through Europe from 1415 to 1417 to attempt to bring the Hundred Years' War to an end. He was not successful.

[128]From 1240 to 1480.

[129]It could be upheld, on the basis of many facts, that there has always been more affinity between the English and the Germans than between the Germans and the French. It has been rather hidden since the Entente Cordiale, but it might suddenly reappear someday.

[130]The example of an economic hegemony founded on political domination was given by Hitler, who during the war set production and export quotas, prices, and exchange rates for the countries he controlled. The U.S.S.R. controls the economy of its satellites by analogous methods.

[131]German trade, in full expansion, has turned not only toward little Europe, but also toward the whole world. The Germans may feel that Europe is too narrow a field of action for them and that by concentrating on it they may be closing a part of the world market against themselves. A large part of German trade is carried on today with Europe, but precisely for that reason the possibilities that other countries offer her might no doubt be greater.

Conclusion

THOSE living after 1870 have often thought that a fundamental opposition prevented any accord between France and Germany, an opposition founded on the character, history, and national claims and ambitions of two peoples; it condemned them irrevocably to enmity, war, and those political combinations which would allow them to win wars.

Were France and Germany really hereditary enemies? For long periods of time they lived in peace, back to back rather than face to face. When they came to blows, it was before the time of Napoleon at least, the wars of kings and not of peoples—prestige rivalries, the appetite for conquest proper to all sovereigns, not particularly to French and German sovereigns. And the history of their territorial quarrels is very simple.

257

Lotharingia, which they quarreled over after the division of Charlemagne's empire, is no more French than it is German; it contained mixed populations. The German Carolingian assigned it to himself first because he was the stronger, but when superiority passed to the king of France, he took in turn from the German emperor the three Bishoprics (French), Alsace (Germanic), a part of Flanders (Dutch), and Lorraine (French). Franche-Comté (French) was taken from the Hapsburgs of Spain, after having belonged to the Hapsburgs of Austria.

In these realignments of territories, it is always France who wins, never the emperor, who is too weak. It is pointless to accuse either people of aggression. The law of might makes right worked here as everywhere else; it was still working in 1870 when Germany would take the upper hand once the balance of power had been changed again.

For the kings of France it was never Germany who was the enemy, but the emperor, especially after the advent of the Hapsburgs, who at certain times had more non-German than German subjects. The king and the French nobility liked to consider themselves as of German origin. When Francis I was a candidate for the empire against Charles V, he called his competitor Spanish, adding in his manifesto, "The French nation conforms in everything to the German; and it has come from the German nation."

What is generally less noticed is the fact that the former Lotharingia, divided little by little according to the hazard of wars, fell only partially to France and to Germany. Its most heavily populated provinces, the richest ones, became independent and today form Belgium, the Netherlands, and Luxembourg. In short, France and Germany, two big nations, have quarreled for centuries to create small states which might have been French or German (they could have been divided without war between France and Germany).[132] They are happy today to belong to neither. La Fontaine expressed the lesson of this history in his fable, "The Thieves and the Ass":

> The ass is sometimes a poor province,
> The thieves are one king and another . . .
> And often by neither of them is the province won.

It required three wars for Germany to retrieve Alsace–Lorraine and lose it again, three for France to lose it but to get it back again. Millions of men, several times more than the population of the region, fell on both sides, and immeasurable wealth was wasted. Can we believe that the French and Germans have finally understood? The simple comparison of dates shows that if they go on this way, they are rushing toward a catastrophe that cannot be prevented. Victories and defeats alternate with growing rapidity: 1870, victory of Germany; 1918, France; 1940, Germany; 1945, France. The intervals are respectively forty-five years, twenty-two, then five years. Isn't this what a modern historian calls "the acceleration of history"? The conflicts, as they grow closer together, grow more murderous. The next conflict will undoubtedly result in the total extermination of both peoples; it would be pointless, for they have no quarrel. Could force of habit be so great that they have to commit double suicide for nothing?

Another difficulty remains. What are we to do with this history which they drag behind them like heavy baggage, this "glorious" heritage which is to justify them and their ancestors? Are we to say that these ancestors were mistaken, that they acted like quarrelsome, stupid children, with this aggravating circumstance, that children's fights do little damage, while those of France and Germany have caused enormous damage? A look at little Switzerland, where Germans and French have been living side by side for centuries, shows that these two peoples can get along with each other, provided they make a little effort. Switzerland is more prosperous than France or Germany; but, the "glory seekers" will cry, it is only a tiny state—isn't greatness worth paying for?

Although this greatness may have been an attribute of Germany as it was of France in the past, it seems to belong definitely to that past. In the dimensions of today's world, France and Germany are no longer and cannot be great nations. A policy of "greatness" would be as fatal for the one as for the other.

It is, however, difficult to uproot the tenacious principle according to which France is said to have defended herself against Germany, or Germany against France—each in his own eyes having always been peaceful, the neighbor always the aggressor. It is understood in these arguments that the Germans are Pan-Germanists and born militarists, while the French are inveterate nationalists revenge seekers, and colonialists. It would be a sad thing indeed if the weight of the past were bearable only at the cost of falsehood. Let us admit, rather, and it will be more manly and more truthful to do it, that the French and the Germans have fought, because men being what they are—quarrelsome, dominating, avid for the property of others—they could do nothing else. Let us remember also that in other countries, people have generally done the same thing. And let us not misunderstand the virtues of courage, endurance, and sacrifice which the most sterile struggles can produce.

Let each then preserve the cult of his heroes and his victories, if we think that school children need examples and that national continuity needs markers for the time which preceded us. Jeanne d'Arc still would be Jeanne d'Arc even if it were proven that France would have done better to ally herself to England. Frederick will always be the Great, even if we think that Austria would have been preferable to Prussia as the unifier of Germany.[133]

Let us consider rather the future, not that distant future which escapes our view, but that in which our own action may develop, a period of about a quarter of a century. What can France and Germany do in this immediate future?

Both have adhered to the Atlantic alliance and European union, two closely linked formations, but which have not yet found their individual law nor the just relationship which ought to exist between them.

We talk of completing the European Community of the Six by an association with other European countries and by a political organization. Aren't these two complements contradictory? Don't they imply different concepts of Europe? If she continues to grow on the economic plane, it isn't certain that she will draw together politically and inversely.

France and Germany

The Germans sometimes seem to hesitate between the two tendencies; it might be that France will lean toward neither and will prefer to be satisfied with the status quo, which would risk weakening Germany's attachment to Europe, especially if circumstances drive her to reunification.

The political-military reorganization of NATO and the reforming of its armies in reference to atomic weapons are problems in which Germany and France will be intimately involved, not alone, however, and without necessarily having identical views. It isn't a foregone conclusion that the relations of Europe and the United States will always remain the same. America could withdraw from Europe, if she thought her economic situation required it, and if the military situation permitted it—if, for example, a certain reduction of tension between her and the U.S.S.R. should occur.

For the moment, the reunification of Germany appears indeed to belong to a rather distant future. We must not, however, forget the possibility of a surprise. If the reunification were to modify the European status of Germany, France is the one country which, by its location, could best get along with it. A Franco–German entente could not give alarm to suspicious minds and would threaten no one. As France would still be the neighbor of the reunited Germany, she could maintain more intimate relations with her than could the other powers. She could be a last point of support for her, the link still uniting her with the west.

Unification under those more or less revolutionary conditions would require a refocussing of Franco–German relations, not their reversal or anesthetization. Can we hope that the spirit which reigns today between the two peoples would permit this accomodation? It would take resolve and initiative on both sides, and trust in the partner. It is clear that the accord would be easier, if Germany remained what she is now in constitution, alliances, and associations. But it is not France's role to choose what its neighbor shall be tomorrow; it is up to the Germans to choose between a West Germany and a united Germany. France can only conform to that choice, adapting her policy to it.

Whatever the future, both will have to make an effort to understand each other. Tolerating each other out of lassitude, because neither desires any more fighting, or because fighting costs too much, is not enough. They must know why they have fought and they must know that the reasons which explain why they have fought no longer exist; that people's needs and dispositions change and that their characters are modified, that an enmity in the past does not prevent a close collaboration in the present.

The German has long been thought of as an impenitent nationalist, a poor democrat; the Frenchman has been called a fanatical democrat. Wouldn't it be rather the other way around today? The German, after his totalitarian regime, is taking a cure in democracy; the Frenchman, tired of his watery democracy, may take the cure through an attack of nationalism. Let both learn to pay little heed to these vicissitudes; neither knows what he will be tomorrow.

Already, however, all kinds of exchanges, economic, cultural, and personal are growing. The French–German treaty of January 22, 1963, should develop them. They show a psychological rapprochement which is going on between France and Germany, and they provide its means of expression.[134] We already have more than a hundred twinships or pairings of French and German cities. Other figures record the improvement in public feeling. They still show a certain resisistance to rapprochement, a resistance justified by the memories of two wars and by the losses which millions of families suffered. When half the French declare themselves in favor of an understanding with Germany, that is already enough to furnish their government a basis for its policy.[135] By basing our will on this feeling, by substituting acts for gestures which are too often hesitant, we shall soon have transformed this half into an incontestable majority.

The vanity of conflict once having been demonstrated and felt, the French and the Germans must not live beside each other, separated by a wall of mistrust and pride, each jealously eyeing the other's superior achievements or qualities, gloating over the other's weaknesses and trying to camouflage or deny his own. Germany has built three times as many housing units as France, for example, and it would be bad grace to argue the point; we could have done as much, if we had taken the trouble. Let us rather draw a lesson from it. It is fitting that between two peoples whose differences are great, but who must consider each other as equals, a frank competition should be evident in all sectors; that each should learn from the other what he lacks and should note the successes on the other side only in order to try to surpass them. The two peoples will have to face each other in peace as they have in war; the victories will no longer belong to the one

264

who will have assembled the most men, the best arms, the most capable strategists or the most numerous allies, but to the one who will have used more invention and endurance, more intelligence and audacity, and who, in social competition, will have shown itself more humane and more generous.

[132]As a matter of fact, Lotharingia, after the death of Lothair II, whose fief it had been, was divided under the Treaty of Mersen in 870 between the eastern Carolingian king, or Germany, and the western one, or France. This division lasted only a few years, since both sovereigns wanted to take it over completely.

[133]It is superfluous to add that the glories of the past are sometimes common to the two peoples, and even to a third partner, Italy. In the course of her history, France has had two emperors—the first, Charlemagne, was German; the second, Napoleon, was Italian. "My status as an Italian," he said, "may have helped a great deal in determining the pope to crown me." (See Marcel Bertrand, *Cahiers de Sainte-Hélène.*)

France rightfully claims kinship with Charlemagne because France was the center of his empire, and with Napoleon because, a year after his birth, Corsica became French, and because he always considered himself as the emperor of the French. These facts could not efface the origins of our great men.

[134]We must note here the effort made by German and French history teachers to discuss together the history of the two countries in order to free it of certain nationalistic excesses and to reach agreement on common broad lines acceptable to all.

People may be surprised to learn that the first attempt in this direction goes back to 1935, under Hitler; it was difficult for it to succeed. It was taken up again in 1950 at Fribourg, and, in 1951, at the Sorbonne and in Mainz, and it resulted in an excellent account of the most debated points of

Franco–German history. All that remains to be done is that these conclusions be applied to the school children's textbooks and to the professors' teaching. This may take time.

[135]A poll taken in May, 1956, by the French Institute of Public Opinion and published in the magazine *Réalités* gave in answer to the question, "Are you for or against a Franco–German rapprochement?": 49 per cent for, 35 per cent against, 16 per cent with no opinion.

To the question, "What are, in your opinion, the areas in which we might begin to reach an understanding with Germany?": 38 per cent answered that it was in the area of economics, 31 per cent thought that the two countries should reach agreement directly, 22 per cent that they should participate in a general European organization.

A more recent sampling, set up in 1959 by the Paris Statisical and Sampling Service, repeated the question asked in 1957 and gave the following results which permit comparisons. Given below are the percentages of affirmative answers to each question in 1957 and in 1959:

Question	1957	1959
Have the Germans understood the errors of the past?	24%	31%
Does Germany sincerely want to cooperate with France?	47	58
Are the German people still dangerous?	72	70
Is Germany a true democracy?	36	42
Can the spirit of domination in Germany cause a catastrophe?	67	63
Can a strong Germany be a danger for France?	63	57
Are economic relations, as close as they possibly can be, desirable between the two countries?	77	80
Must Germany become an ally and friend for France?	68	70

Perhaps we should set opposite those figures the results of a poll conducted in Germany and in West Berlin in 1953 and in 1959. It was based on a single question, really quite different from the questions above: "With what countries do you think we should collaborate closely?" Following are the percentages of affirmative answers:

Country	1953	1959
United States	83%	81%
Great Britain	62	49
France	55	48
U.S.S.R.	18	31
Poland	11	25
Israel	15	19

Index

René Lauret, and eminent French journalist, is the author of several books (*Raymond Poincaré; Les Conditions de la vie en Allemagne; Le Théatre allemand d'aujourd'hui; Le Trois Grands et la bombe atomique; Faites travailler l'Allemagne;* and *Causes de guerre, chances de paix*). This is his first volume to appear in English. He studied at the Universities of Montpellier, Nancy, Paris, Leipzig and Munich, and was a professor in Le Havre and Paris. An interpreter in the British Army during the First World War, he returned to journalism and was President of the Foreign Press Association. During the Second World War, he was the Press Attaché in the French Embassy in Bern. An editor for the *Bulletin de l'Étranger* and on the editorial staff of *Le Monde* from 1944 to 1953, M. Lauret is now retired and lives in Paris. Among his many honorary awards are Officer of the Legion of Honor (France) and Knight of the Order of Merit, First Class (Germany).